Asteroids in Astrology Simplified

"Sky Don't Lie" ~ Courtney Cruthirds-Schmiedlin

Copyright Courtney Cruthirds-Schmiedlin, 2025
All Rights Reserved

Without limiting the rights reserved above under copyright, no part of this publication may be reproduced, stored in, or introduced into a retrieval system, or transmitted in any form or by any means (electronic, mechanical, photocopying, scanning, recording or otherwise), without written permission from both the author and the publisher, except in the case of brief quotations embodied in reviews and articles.

The scanning, uploading and distribution of this book via the Internet, or via any other means, without the written permission of the publisher is illegal and punishable by law. Please do not encourage electronic piracy of copyrighted materials.
ISBN: 978-0-86690-698-2
Requests and inquiries may be mailed to the publisher:
American Federation of Astrologers, Inc.
6553 S. Rural Road
Tempe, AZ 85283

www.astrologers.com

Table of Contents:

Introduction	v
How to find asteroids in your natal chart	vi

Part 1 - Themed Lists of Asteroids

1.	Cosmic Connection	1
2.	Positivity	7
3.	Birds	13
4.	Sleep and Dreams	22
5.	Justice and Law	25
6.	Asian	27
7.	Time Related	31
8.	Alice in Wonderland	33
9.	Weather and Natural Disaster	35
10.	Moon	38
11.	Business and Fortune	40
12.	Death Related	42
13.	Time- Dimensional Travel	45
14.	Norse/Celt Mythology	49
15.	Prophetic Gift	59
16.	LGBTQ	63
17.	Lilith	67
18.	Love, Lust, and Sex	68
19.	Mysticism and Magic	77
20.	Fairytale and Fictional Characters	82
21.	Depression and Suicide	93
22.	Nefarious and Violence Theme	96
23.	Health, Healing, and Medical	100
24.	Miscellaneous	104
25.	Numerology and Synchronicity	111
26.	Indigenous	115
27.	Vedic	117
28.	Egyptian	120
29.	Religious, Spiritual, and Saints	122
30.	Artistic and Philosophical	127
31.	Most Popular	136

Part 2- Individual Asteroid Deep Dives and Case Studies

1. Sauron — 139
2. Empedocles — 144
3. Polybius — 146
4. Memnon — 148
5. Xenocrates and The Fates — 149
6. Admetos - Case Study — 152
7. Beowulf — 154
8. The Hare, Ostara, and the Egg — 155
9. Asteroid Guedes AKA Papa Legba — 159
10. Marie Laveau- Case Study — 161
11. Einstein - Case Study — 164
12. The Three Furies — 166
13. Nut — 167
14. Hathor/Athor — 168
15. Pholus — 169
16. Herodias — 170
17. Dione — 171
18. Baby Eve - Case Study — 172

Part 3- List of Personal Name Asteroids — 175

Introduction

Astrology traditionally focuses on the planets, but asteroids provide an additional, personalized layer of insight.

Asteroids are like the garnishments or the jewelry we wear in our natal charts. They highlight areas of interest by adding an extra layer of depth to a reading. They can be used to find something hidden, obscured or not easily seen just by reading a chart alone. Using them to track transits is especially helpful in gaining additional insights into an event or unexpected behaviors. My mission is to make asteroids easier to use by having them in easy to navigate lists. Currently, there are over 25,000 asteroids in the database. This can be extremely overwhelming to navigate, my hope is to make working with asteroids less intimidating.

It is important to note that the orb limit for asteroids is very tight. The standard is a 1-3-degree orb for conjunctions and other aspects. Larger asteroids (some called dwarf planets) such as Chiron, Ceres, Pallas, Vesta, Juno could be granted a wider 5-degree orb. In fact, Chiron has been given up to an 8-degree orb of consideration for some.

The length of time it takes for certain asteroids to move through the signs is also important. Just like the planets, some move fast like Venus or mars, while others take several years like Neptune or Pluto.

There are many additional layers to peel back in this niche field of study. For example, understanding the difference between asteroids and hypothetical points. Hamburg (hypothetical) points or trans-Neptunian objects. The research is still relatively new and evolving. Opinions vary greatly in these matters and my main objective has always been to remain open to constant in-flux changes, ideas, and beliefs.

Trigger warning*: this book mentions several sensitive topics, such as death, suicide, sexual references and abuse. Extreme violence and murder.*

How to find asteroids in the natal chart:

How to find asteroids in your own chart using astro dot com. (www.astro.com) website.

Step 1: Go to "extended chart selection"

Step 2: Scroll all the way down to the bottom where you see "additional objects" and open the box where it says "manual entry".

It is in this box you will enter the numbers that are typed next to each asteroid listed.

Each asteroid must be entered manually by number.

See photo for reference.

Additional objects

Common elements:

0 Items

Selection from following lists:

- Asteroid name/number list with 24836 names
- List of fixed stars
- List of other horoscope factors and "hypothetical" planets

Manual entry:

You can enter the objects as a comma-separated list. For asteroids use their official catalogue numbers, for fixed stars their names, and for other objects their list numbers according to the link given below, e.g. "433,227,Sirius,Regulus,h21,h22,h48". Altogether, the limit is 30 additional objects.

PART 1: Themed Lists

Cosmic Connection

369 Aeria: air, one of the four classic elements. Also known as "wind". Air is sometimes linked to intelligence and psyche. Blood was associated with air, because it is both hot and wet. The archangel of air is Raphael. Sometimes considered the "life force" or "sky breath". Spoken prayers or spells.

2432 Soomana: "Star Girl" in Hopi.

2433 Sootiyao: "Star Boy" in Hopi.

2938 Hopi: Hopi Indian myths, legends and folktales. Many connect with the Hopi prophecy. The blue star Kachina, according to the Hopi mythology, is a spirit that signify the coming of the beginning of a new world, and the spirit appears in the form of a blue star. That is the ninth and final sign before the "Day of Purification", which is the day the old world is destroyed and a new one begins. They are cosmically linked to aliens or outer space. Could indicate a territorial dispute.

9669 Symmetria: symmetry or togetherness; may indicate crop circles and using symbols to communicate. Being balanced. Symmetrical.

5881 Akashi: Akashic Records. Cosmic lifetime, karmic guide.

3243 Skytel: Sky + telescope, communication with the cosmos; gathering cosmic intelligence.

13111 Papacosmos: "Sky Father".

25000 Astrometria: astrometry involves precise measurements of the positions and movements of stars and other celestial bodies. Used to sky map stars and galaxies for star catalogues.

35734 Dilithium: (Star Trek) is an invented material which serves as a controlling agent in the faster-than-light warp drive. Creates high frequency electromagnetic fields.

7861 Messenger: communications, send and receive messages.

4246 Telemann: messenger, make contact. Communication, reception, deliver.

59800 Astropis: astronomy or astrology. "Astro piece".

8719 Vesmir: cosmos, creation, space, universe, outer space.

37556 Svyaztie: svyaz and tie, Russian and English word combo meaning "connection". Honoring the astronomical collaborations and friendships between the two countries.

Keywords: foreign connection or bond; teamwork; beyond boundaries.

344000 Astropolis: having to do with astronomy or astrology. Passionate about planets, outer space exploration.

71001 Natspasoc: stands for "National Space Society".

Keywords: having to do with outer space. Astronomy. Scientific sky research. Astrology. Cosmic connection to space.

11911 Angel: Divine messenger; guardian; protection.

20000 Varuna: the great cosmic equalizer.

4255 Spacewatch: watching the cosmos, using cosmic time.

620 Drakonia: Draconic Constellation, dragons coiling around the north pole. Spans over 250 degrees in the zodiac, from Aries to Sagittarius and contains eighteen fixed stars.

25115 Drago: dragon; Draconian; Draco constellation, (as above).

100000 Astronautica: to sail in the sky. Space craft. Means "star sailor" in Latin. Astronauts.

8039 Grandprisim: psychic awareness through shapes or geometry. Cosmic crystal connection.

8958 Stargazer: watch the stars, following the constellations.

343444 Halluzinelle: named after a robot hologram in a German science fiction TV show. Possibly having something to do with robots, outer space. It could be someone who has a very futuristic outlook. Someone who is "way ahead of time". Possibly good with technology, and a vision of where/how mankind will evolve.

30 Urania: goddess of astronomy and astrology. "Astro goddess".

4001 Ptolemy: Greek astronomer and astrologer; famous for his interpretations of the fixed stars and constellations. Prominent in astrologers' or astronomers' charts. Could also represent a person who specializes in cartography.

132 Aethra: means "bright sky". She is sometimes called the wife of Atlas and mother of the Pleiades (the seven sisters), Hyades (more usually the offspring of Pleione), and Hyas. Aethra is also a fictional moon in the Colony Wars franchise.

Keywords: star/sky mother; associated with rain. The constellation and star seed origins of the Pleiades located in the Taurus constellation 29 Taurus - 01 Gemini.

1198 Atlantis: starseed connections; past life recall.

H56 White Moon Selene: Moon goddess, (this is the hypothetical point).

580 Selene: asteroid Selene (Moon goddess).

1154 Astronomia: considered to be an "astrologers" asteroid. Study of astrology or astronomy. "Astro maniac"; fanatical about the sky.

10412 Tsukuyomi: Japanese Moon god. Also called "Moon reader".

308798 Teo: means "god".

4003 Schumann: Earth's heartbeat; frequencies.

15332 CERN: They have a huge particle collider that opens portals and focuses on "dark" anti-matter. Also linked to time travel or astral projection, remote viewing.

3325 TARDIS: Time and Relative Dimension in Space (fictional time machine). Astral Projection. Time and space travel. Remote viewing.

2089 Cetacea: ancient order of whales, dolphins and large sea creatures. The Inuits believed whales to be sacred messengers. Communicating with the whales was the equivalent to communicating with the gods. People with star seed origins from the Cetus constellation: between Aries and Taurus containing twenty fixed stars.

9172 Abhramu: white elephant cloud goddess. Cloud messenger.

59 Elpis: spirit of hope or expectation. Spirit to summon or pray to, receive hopeful messages. Surprise. Last item released from Pandora's box.

57424 Caelumnoctu: "The sky at night" in Latin.

7192 Cieletspace: Means "sky and space" in French.

Keywords: space time, space origins, star seed connections, astronomy, astrology.

2909 Hoshi-no-ie: means "star house". Possible meaning, where is your "star home" constellation or origins?

14566 Hokule'a : Hawaiian word for fixed star Arcturus. For reference, Fixed star Arcturus is at 24 Libra in the Bootes Constellation. Arcturus is seen as the "protector".

18132 Spector: specter means a ghostly apparition, a ghost, or simply an idea that people find frightening. Visible incorporeal spirit, especially one of a terrifying nature; phantom; apparition. Some object or source of terror or dread i.e., the specter of disease or famine. Supernatural phenomenon; haunts; haunting thoughts; induce fear. If aspected or in transition with the South Node it may look like "ghosts of the past" memories. If it is conjunct Neptune, it may show many supernatural experiences.

22540 Mork: slang term for aliens in the British science fiction television series The Aliens. Alien or extraterrestrial sightings.

22003 Startek: being connected to the stars; possible star seed connection if located next to a prominent fixed star in the natal chart. To shine; illuminate.

200025 Cloudgate: sky portal or bridge between realms; heavenly gate; cosmic cloud computing.

2244 Tesla: space technology, communications and transportation. Starlink Satellite Systems.

24626 Astrowizard: asteroid for "astrologers".

6465 Zvezdotchet: means "star gazer" in Russian. (It's a magazine for astronomers.) The google the translation says it means "astrologer".

Keywords: star gazer, astrology, astrologer, astronomy.

11144 Radiocommunicata: radio communications and frequencies.

50000 Quaoar: cosmic creation and origins. Spiritual discovery/journey. Could be considered challenging when being hit by a transit leading to personal transformations or belief changes.

233 Asterope: part of the Pleiades. Name means "lightening" spark of inspiration striking randomly. "Seeing the light." Asterope is also a fixed star in the Pleiades constellation, part of the seven sisters. Possible star seed connection; located at 29 Taurus- 01 Gemini.

1067 Lunaria: means "moon shaped" and "honesty". Connected to the Moon.

32770 Starchik: Star chick (girl), possibly strong in charts of famous child stars.

4150 Starr: The stars; possibly literal "movie stars".

10831 Takamagahara: heavens; floating bridge to heaven; bridge between worlds.

731 Sorga: Indonesian for "heavens". "Gateway to Heaven."

1819 Laputa: "castle in the sky", dream house.

29080 Astrocourier: astro messenger; astrologer or astronaut.

10216 Popastro: Popular astronomy/astrology; astrology "couture" or culture.

1252 Celestia: heavenly, or "of the sky". Space. Astronomical, extraterrestrial, stellar, astral, planetary, "a celestial body".

11365 NASA: space exploration.

2365 Interkosmos: interplanetary space program; space exploration.

658 Asteria: goddess of nocturnal oracles, and falling/shooting stars.

8589 Stellaris: space exploration; contact with extraterrestrials; interstellar.

20461 Dioretsa: "asteroid" spelled backwards, "as above so below".

21073 Darksky: night sky; darkness; background for the stars.

274020 Skywalker: fictional character from the "Star Wars" movies. Could take the name literally as "Sky Walker". One who walks with the stars in the sky. Astral projection. Space travel.

6669 Obi: Obi-Wan Kenobi from the Star Wars movies. A legendary Jedi master, Obi-Wan Kenobi was a wise, noble man, and gifted in the ways of the Force.

4047 Chang'E: Chinese Moon goddess and immortality. She is also associated with space travel.

On the full Moon night of the eighth lunar month, an open-air altar is set up facing the Moon for the worship of Chang'e. New pastries are put on the altar for her to bless. She is said to endow her worshippers with beauty.

This is also the name of the space craft that the Chinese have landed on the far side of the Moon.

332 Siri: the iPhone navigation and assistance artificial intelligence named "Siri"; virtual assistant.

Keywords: where/how one gets help or assistance; technology; navigational/communication bridge between technology and humanity.

1838 Ursa: means "bear". The bear symbolism is vast. The Big Dipper and Little Dipper constellations are called "Ursa Major" and "Ursa Minor". Considering this, I would be curious to research possible star seed origins if this asteroid lands in those constellations in one's chart. The bear symbolizes strength and is widely respected in native cultures as a shamanic spirit of protection, courage, and wisdom.

12711 Tukmit: "Father Sky", god in the Luiseno creation story, who bore the First People. Orgins; ancestry. Cultural appropriation; giving and taking.

1347 Patria: Latin for "fatherland". Heaven, regarded as the true home from which the soul is exiled while on Earth.

Note: use this asteroid with DNA #55555 to show one's cosmic and earthly "roots". Look for connections with the Nodes and the MC/IC.

Don't forget the black holes and galactic centers:
- 26-27 Sagittarius - Galactic Center.
- 0-1 Libra - Super Galactic Center.
- 14 Sagittarius - The Great Attractor.

Positivity

Sometimes, we get caught up only looking for bad, and the good goes unnoticed. Keep in mind, the asteroids are interchangeable in meaning and interpretation too. This means we need to use our own intuition at times to feel out the asteroid and what it means for us personally. There isn't one set definition.

11911 Angel: Divine intervention; guardian angel.

965 Angelica: angelic and translated in Greek to "messenger" (Angelos).

8990 Compassion: compassionate; empathy; comfort.

31 Euphrosyne: goddess of joy, good cheer, and mirth (laughter).

32 Pomona: goddess of fruitful abundance.

79 Eurynome: peace, unity, and balance.

3548 Eurybates: known for his honesty and faithfulness as a squire to Odysseus.

Keywords: loyal, honest, helpful or providing services. Kind and reliable. Assistance. Support.

3757 Anagolay: is the goddess of lost things in Ancient Philippine Tagalog mythology.

Keywords: things that are hidden, lost, or hard to find. Recovering lost items. Reunited. Something or someone missing. I also wonder if this is where we can figuratively "find ourselves" or rediscover something "lost" within ourselves. *She can be useful using transits in missing persons cases.*

639 Latona: protectress of young, also goddess of modesty.

1288 Santa: saint.

7292 Prosperin: prosper, thrive, flourish, do well.

29672 Salvo: save, salvation; safety net.

11790 Goode: goodness, wholesome.

32761 Porta Coeli: Gate to Heaven; happiness and enlightenment.

9395 Saintmichael: Saint Michael or Archangel Michael; guardian, protector; also associated with fixed star Aldebaran "Watcher of the east".

296577 Arkhangelsk: guardian, archangel.

64 Angelina: angelic, angel.

799 Gudula: The Saint Gudula of Brabant; depicted as a woman with a lantern that the devil tries to blow out. (Illumination and protection.)

125 Liberatrix: liberate, freedom, release. Break free from something holding you back. ***Note:*** *good to look at the transit for this one.*

8732 Champion: victory, winning, to achieve, advocate, supporter, defender.

14959 Triumf: triumph, victorious, joyous, success.

18601 Zafar: means victory.

12 Victoria: Roman goddess of victory.

700 Auravictrix: Latin for "victory against the wind".

Keywords: beating the odds, hard earned victory.

17494 Antaviana: a symbol of solidarity, responsibility, freedom and hope.

145 Adeona: Roman goddess of protection and safe return. She is sometimes compared to the nature of Juno (protectress of children). Her name comes from the Latin verb adeo, "to approach or visit" as well as "take possession of one's inheritance".

Keywords: protect children; teach, guide and provide for all children. Brings home lost children; possible indication of adoption in one's chart. Safety during travel.

1583 Antilochus: hero from the Trojan war. He was distinguished for his beauty, swiftness of foot, and skill as a charioteer. He was a great commander who performed many deeds of valor. He was a favorite of the gods and close friend to Achilles.

When his father Nestor was attacked, Antilochus sacrificed himself to save him, thus fulfilling an oracle which had warned to "beware of an Ethiopian".

Keywords: war hero. Skilled leader. Physically fit. Honorable. A place where we may sacrifice ourselves for someone or something else. Fulfilling something fated. Saving a life. Well respected. Knowing when to lay down your sword and accept fate.

8124 Guardi: guardian; protector.

4390 Madreteresa: Mother Teresa, protection.

2307 Garuda: is generally a protector with power to swiftly go anywhere, ever watchful, and an enemy of the serpent. Wards off evil.

1061 Paeonia: peony flower that symbolizes romance, prosperity, good fortune, a happy marriage, riches, honor, and compassion. Peonies can also mean bashfulness.

838 Seraphina: guardian angel or Saint Serafina who cares for physically challenged people.

258 Tyche: goddess of luck.

Note: *good for transits.*

652 Jubilatrix: rejoice, gleeful, joyful expression.
3561 Divine: heavenly; angelic; delightful; spiritual; karmically linked.
47 Aglaja: goddess of beauty, splendor, glory, magnificence, and adornment.
8992 Magnanimity: generosity, virtue, kindness, understanding, grace, genuine goodness and compassion. A little kindness goes a long way.
19019 Sunflower: symbolism of the sunflower is to bring joy; adoration, loyalty and longevity.
567 Eleutheria: liberty, freedom.
7 Iris: divine rainbow goddess and messenger of the gods. Luck. She is connected to the oak of truth. The "ideal" messenger goddess who can travel between the heavens and the earth at blinding speeds carrying messages from god to god. Connected to the concept of unity, "to unite" or "to join". She is the seventh asteroid discovered (hence her number) which corresponds to the seven colors of the chakras, seven colors of the rainbow, seven days a week, seven seas, seven continents, and the seven traditional planets. Seven is considered the luckiest number. She could relate to spiritual completeness and perfection through the recognition of the union of the physical number four and the spiritual number three. Prominent in the seed of life itself. Iris has a twin sister named Arke(no asteroid), however, she is an important piece of the equation. Arke was the other side of the "bridge", acting as the anchor or tether to earth while Iris astral travelled.
410 Chloris: goddess of flowers and spring: equivalent to Flora. Represents new growth; blooming; fresh; revived; fresh start.
134 Sophrosyne: is an Ancient Greek concept of an ideal of excellence of character and soundness of mind, which when combined in one well-balanced individual leads to other qualities, such as temperance, moderation, prudence, purity, decorum and self-control.
432971 Loving: care deeply about; comfort; secure warmth.
12718 Le Gentil: helpful; kind; pleasant; nice; likable; gentile; polite; respectful.
200 Dynamene: means "she who can", or "capable one". Competent. Confidence.
23 Thalia: muse of comedy; the joyous or flourishing one; happiness.
7899 Joya: joy, elation, happiness, something to celebrate.
92891 Bless : where one is blessed or receives blessings.

424 Gratia: grace, gracious, gratitude, thankful.

5081 Sanguin: optimistic or positive, especially in an apparently bad or difficult situation. Hopeful. Enthusiastic.

708 Raphaela: Archangel Raphael (he who heals). Physical or emotional healing. Sometimes associated with the royal fixed star Regulus.

1908 Pobeda: Russian for "victory". Success. Win. Accomplish.

1052 Belgica: Celtic for bravery, courage, and conflict.

1846 Bengt: means "blessing".

14500 Kibo: means "hope, hopeful, or wish" in Japanese.

66 Maja: Maia, Great Mother Earth goddess who represents passion, wishes, and playfulness. Maja is also the name of the goddess in Greek mythology, known as the most beautiful among the seven sisters in Pleiades. She is connected to the growing strength of nature (springtime). Often associated with eagles and mountains.

60000 Miminko: Czech word that expresses the innocence of the very beginning of human life.

Keywords: innocence; purity; clarity; of pure heart and intent.

6568 Serendip: Serendipity. The occurrence and development of events by chance in a happy or beneficial way.

Keywords: "leave it to the wind" attitude. Stop fighting to control the outcome. When unexpected surprises arrive, let the magic in!

475 Ocllo: Inca queen goddess; wife of the creator god of civilization in Inca mythology. Mother of fertility and motherhood. She taught the other village women how to spin thread, sew, cook etc.

Keywords: personified as the ideal housewife and mother. Civilized manors. Hospitality; nurturing; motherhood; teachers; community service.

1292 Luce: means "light"; finding your way through darkness.

3642 Frieden: German for "peace" or reconciliation.

975 Perseverantia: meaning "perseverance", never give up. To push through many difficulties to reach a goal or achieve success. To endure great struggle for great reward. Dedication. Discipline.

37530 Dancing Angel: guardian angel of joy and celebration. Could indicate dancers or performers. Someone who finds happiness in music or concerts.

3015 Candy: something sweet. In Latin the name means "dazzling bright shining light". Cheerful. "Eye candy" or something pleasant to the senses. Brings happiness.

22622 Strong: strength; support system; courage; vigor; inner-strength; fortitude and bravery. In tarot, the Strength card.

172 Baucis: mythological Greek woman who along with her husband welcomed in disguised gods, Zeus and Hermes, into their home- thus representing hospitality.

Keywords: hospitable; working in hospitality industry; gracious, humble, kindness; generosity.

5073 Junttura: embodies the Finnish mentality to get things done, stubbornly and at *all* costs. Never give up.

Shadow side: commit illegal activity to achieve results.

8061 Gaudium: Latin for "joy, pleasure, and delight". It is designed to compensate the gloom of Melancholia #5708.

1201 Strenua: was a goddess of the new year, purification, and well-being. The goddess who made a person "vigorous and strong". Diligent and careful. Healthy habits. Beginnings.

1459 Magnya: means "clear, bright, wonderful" when translated from Latin to Russian. "With great distinction." Great and remarkable attributes.

37452 Spirit: inner soul urge; consciousness; spirituality; pure essence of the soul. If in harsh aspect with the Nodes or Chiron it could represent a subconscious fear of failure in this life.

6151 Viget: comes from the motto for Prinston University: "Del Sub Numine Viget" or "under the power of God she flourishes".

Keywords: a place to find Divine enlightenment and knowledge. Where one thrives and prospers. The origins of this phrase can go deep. You unlock the secret passage for which is still used in dark initiation rituals today. Secrecy; finding the light; in need of protection.

4339 Almamater: "Alma mater" used to describe the university one attended. In Latin "alma = nourishing/kind/soul"; "mater= mother". Some have made the connection to the goddess Cybele; "ultimate mother".

Keywords: receiving knowledge/wisdom; kindness; nourishment; education; a place of comfort and growth. If used literally "kind mother".

12016 Green: symbolically is the color of life, renewal, rebirth, spring, nature. Its energy represents growth, harmony, freshness, safety, fertility, and environment. Green is traditionally associated with money, finances, banking, ambition, greed, jealously, and Wall Street.

12032 Ivory: symbol of purity, innocence, cleanliness, a symbol of chastity, opulence and virtue.

1610 Mirnaya: Russian for "peaceful"; an idealist who dreams of living in a harmonious world.

1613 Smiley: smile; happy; feeling joy/humor; optimism. Teeth or dentist.

129234 Silly: comical; funny; lighthearted; humorous; goofy/joking; not serious.

289 Nenetta: French slang for a frivolous woman. Also means favor or grace; not taking anything too serious; playful; lighthearted; silly; no worries.

296 Phaethusa: Greek goddess; daughter of Helios. The personification of the brilliant, blinding rays of the sun. "Radiance." She tended herds of cattle with a copper staff.

Keywords: brilliant; bright; intelligent; beautiful; guardian of nature.

Bird Themes

What if birds chirp in Morse code? They are considered messengers.

8750 Nettarufina: red-crested pochard; large golden red duck.

8751 Nigricollis: black-necked grebe; water bird like a duck.

6790 Pingoiun: an Arctic bird, similar to the penguin of Antarctica. The pingouin that became extinct in Newfoundland in 1844. Not many myths go along with the bird itself. The cute stories we know, how they "mate for life" are romantic indeed. It is interesting that the book publishing empire called "Penguin Books" started in the 1930s. *Could indicate writing or publishing books.*

52387 Huitzilopochtli: is an Aztec god associated with the Sun. His name, meaning "hummingbird of the south", came from the Aztec belief that the spirits of killed warriors followed the sun through the sky during four subsequent years. Thereafter they were transformed into hummingbirds.

Keywords: The hummingbird spirit totem is representative of finding happiness in small things; embracing the present with enthusiasm; ability to fly fast away from negativity; endurance; courage; independence; determination.

60183 Falcone: the fierce falcon has special symbolism and meaning in Egypt where it represented the rising Sun. Many depictions of the gods bore a falcon head, most notably Ra, the solar deity. As the "king" of birds, the falcon represents victory, ruler ship, and overcoming. Like other birds, the falcon also signifies the higher self and connections with the spirit world. Other characteristics ascribed to the falcon include energy, foresight, ambition, fortitude, willpower, transformation, vision, mental acuity, freedom, control, magickal aptitude, and a bright life-force.

8753 Nycticorax: black-crowned night heron. The etymology of "nycticorax" translates to "night raven".

In Norse mythology, it is called "Nachtkrapp," and used in tales to scare children to go to sleep, or terrorize them into silence. It is depicted with no eyes, which if looked into, cause death. It is also depicted with holes in its wings, which cause illness and disease if looked at. Some of the most common legends claim that the Nachtkrapp leaves its hiding place at night to hunt. If it is seen by little children, it will abduct them into its nest and messily devour them. First ripping off their limbs, and then picking out their heart.

According to other legends, the Nachtkrapp will merely put children in his bag and take them away.

Keywords: nocturnal. Psychological sleep paralysis, or an unnatural fear of birds. Suffering with night terrors. Additionally, I would look at it as more of a warning sign or omen to have a personal encounter. And I would be very curious if this asteroid showed strongly in child abduction or death cases in a mother's chart. (Especially as an active transit.) More research needs to be done to confirm this hypothesis.

8754 Leucorodia: is a wading bird of the ibis and spoonbill family.

The African sacred ibis was an object of religious veneration in Ancient Egypt, particularly associated with the deity Djehuty or otherwise commonly referred to in Greek as Thoth. He is responsible for writing, mathematics, measurement and time as well as the Moon and magic! Thoth is popularly depicted as an ibis-headed man in the act of writing.

According to local legend in the Birecik area, the northern bald ibis was one of the first birds that Noah released from the ark as a symbol of fertility.

The African sacred ibis is the unit symbol of the Israeli Special Forces unit known as Unit 212, or Maglan.

According to Josephus, Moses used the ibis to help him defeat the Ethiopians.

Ibis carries a lengthy and strong historical symbolism.

Note: *when Ibis shows up for you, its message should not be ignored. Ibis reminds you of your own power and spirituality, and urges you to look for the answers deep within yourself.*

8757 Cyaneus: hen harrier; bird of prey. Name translates to "circle of flight". I would strongly reflect on the "circle" symbolism as cycles.

In some parts of Europe people believed that seeing a harrier perched on a house was a sign that three people would die.

325973 Cardinal: in many cultures, the red color of cardinals can symbolize good luck and abundance. Cardinals can also represent renewal, transformation, manifestation, new beginnings, domestic harmony, and new or renewed romance.

Note: *if asteroid Cardinal is in one of the cardinal houses of one's natal chart, it would be prudent to follow the transits as Cardinal moves through the chart.*

8758 Perdix: grey partridge. In Greek mythology, Perdix was the sister of Daedalus. She had a son who was so gifted, that Daedalus became jealous of him. He pushed the boy off a tower, but the gods intervened and turned the youth into a partridge before he reached the ground. He has been afraid of heights ever since, which is why partridges always fly so close to the ground. Even at Christmas, partridges never perch in trees.

Keywords: protect the young, preserve youth, creation. Easily adapt in environments that are ever changing. If harshly aspected, it could represent a deep wound from childhood, making a person "freeze" instead of fly from certain situations.

8761 Crane: the cranes' beauty and spectacular mating dances have made them highly symbolic birds in many cultures with records dating back to ancient times.

- The crane was a bird of omen. In the tale of Ibycus and the cranes, a thief attacked Ibycus (a poet of the sixth century BCE) and left him for dead. Ibycus called to a flock of passing cranes, which followed the attacker to a theater and hovered over him until, stricken with guilt, he confessed to the crime.
- Cranes would appoint one of their own to stand guard while they slept. The sentry would hold a stone in its claw, so that if it fell asleep, it would drop the stone and wake. A crane holding a stone in its claw is a well-known symbol in heraldry and is known for its vigilance.
- Greek and Roman myths often portrayed the dance of cranes as a love of joy and a celebration of life; and the crane was often associated with both Apollo and Hephaestus.
- Throughout Asia, the crane is a symbol of happiness and eternal youth. In Japan, the crane is one of the mystical or holy creatures (others include the dragon and the tortoise). And symbolizes good fortune and longevity because of its fabled life span of a thousand years.

Keywords: grace, love, harmony and peace. Protection. Ancient wisdom. Strength. Auspicious. Vigilante. Justice. Happiness. Luck. Dancing. Enjoying the moment. Teamwork. Co-dependence.

8752 Flammeus: short-eared owl. Owls are the most well-known wise messengers in mythology.

8768 Barnowl: See owl info below.

8962 Noctua: means "little owl", associated with Athene.

"Owls have been both feared and venerated, despised and admired, considered wise and foolish, and associated with witchcraft and medicine, the weather, birth and death. Speculation about owls began in earliest folklore, too long ago to date, but passed down by word of mouth over generations."- Source: owlpages.com by Deane Lewis.

"In early Indian folklore, owls represent wisdom, helpfulness, auspicious and have powers of prophecy. This theme recurs in Aesop's fables and in Greek myths and beliefs. By the Middle Ages in Europe, the owl had become the associate of witches and the inhabitant of dark, lonely and profane places, a foolish but feared specter. An owl's appearance at night, when people are helpless and blind, linked them with the unknown, its eerie call filled people with foreboding and apprehension; a death was imminent, or some evil was at hand. During the eighteenth century the zoological aspects of owls were detailed through close observation, reducing the mystery surrounding these birds. With superstitions dying out in the twentieth century, in the West at least, the owl has returned to its position as a symbol of wisdom."

8773 Torquilla: the wryneck (old world woodpeckers). Iynx was the nymph inventor of a magical love-charm known as the lynx, a spinning wheel with a wryneck bird attached. Iynx used her enchantments to make Zeus fall in love with her or some say, with the nymph Io. Hera was enraged and transformed her into a wryneck bird.

Note: the English word "jinx" is derived from Iynx's name.

8774 Viridis: green woodpecker. Woodpeckers are considered lucky birds by many Native Americans, particularly in Western tribes, and are associated with friendship and happiness. In some California Indian tribes, woodpeckers are considered medicine birds, and woodpecker scalps and feathers have traditionally been used to adorn ceremonial objects, headdresses, and dance regalia. Woodpecker is an important clan crest in some Northwest Coast tribes and can sometimes be found carved on totem poles.

8964 Corax: raven. Very strong historically represented messenger. Divine messenger. Prophetic messenger from the gods. They are mediators between the living and the dead. Very auspicious and always carry warnings. *Ravens are also tied to "cleansing" and purging something out of your system to remain healthy.*

8978 Barbatus: bearded vulture. Iranian mythology considers the rare, bearded vulture the symbol of luck and happiness. It was believed that if the shadow of a Homa fell on one, he would rise to sovereignty and anyone shooting the bird would die in forty days.

The Ancient Greeks used them to guide their political decisions. Bearded vultures were one of the few species of birds that could yield valid signs to these soothsayers.

8979 Clanga: spotted eagle (see below.)

8980 Heliaca: imperial eagle (see below.)

The eagle is used in heraldry as a charge, as a supporter, and as a crest. The eagle with its keen eyes symbolized perspicacity, courage, strength and immortality, but is also considered "king of the skies" and messenger of the highest gods. With these attributed qualities the eagle became a symbol of power and strength in Ancient Rome. It has been connected by the Greeks with the god Zeus, by the Romans with Jupiter, by the Germanic tribes with Odin, by the Judeo-Christian in many scriptures.

Keywords: strength, courage, freedom, sacred messengers, seeing everything going on and quickly accessing situations. Vision quests, psychic intuition, mind's 3rd eye. Highest power. Overcoming obstacles.

702 Alauda: larks; from Shakespeare's Sonnet 29: "The lark at break of day arising /From sullen earth, sings hymns at heaven's gate" (11–12). The lark is also (often simultaneously) associated with "lovers and lovers" observance. (Use with the Lovers or Devil tarot card.)

Some say it signifies the "passage from Earth to Heaven and from Heaven to Earth".

706 Hirundo: passerines (songbird). Good luck and new love.

709 Fringilla: finches. Joy, happiness, high vibrational energy. Harmony.

713 Luscinia: nightingales. Because of the violence associated with the myth, the song of the nightingale is often depicted or interpreted as a sorrowful lament. Some say the prophetess Cassandra heard the bird give her, her own fate.

Keywords: prophetic message. Love and sacrifice. Innocence and purity. A fate point in the chart; should be tracked with transits for noteworthy events. Does this asteroid interact with Cassandra #114?

2731 Cucula: cuckoo bird. Cuckoos have played a role in human culture for thousands of years, appearing in Greek mythology as sacred to the goddess Hera. It is usually associated with spring. In India, cuckoos are sacred to Kamadeva, the god of desire and longing. Whereas in Japan, the cuckoo symbolizes unrequited love.

2868 Upupa: hoopoe bird notable for its "crown of feathers". In Persia they are considered the king of birds. There are many biblical references with this bird. And it depends on the area for which myth to go by. For example, Hoopoes were thought of as thieves across much of Europe, and harbingers of war in Scandinavia. In Estonian tradition, hoopoes are strongly connected with death and the underworld; their song is believed to foreshadow death for many people or cattle. In medieval ritual magic, the hoopoe was thought to be an evil bird. The Munich Manual of Demonic Magic, a collection of magical spells compiled in Germany frequently requires the sacrifice of a hoopoe to summon demons and perform other magical intentions.

Note: *dark magic and sorcery are intertwined with this bird in symbolism.*

4471 Graculus: alpine chough, from the crow family. In Greek mythology, the red-billed chough, also known as "sea crow", was considered sacred to the Titan Cronus and dwelt on Calypso's "Blessed Island".

The red-billed chough has a long association with Cornwall and appears on the Cornish coat of arms.

According to Cornish legend, King Arthur did not die after his last battle but rather his soul migrated into the body of a red-billed chough. The red color of its bill and legs being derived from the blood of the last battle and hence killing this bird was unlucky. *Legend also holds that after the last Cornish chough departs from Cornwall, the return of the chough, as happened in 2001, will then mark the return of King Arthur.*

8433 Brachyrhynchus: pink-footed goose. Respect and loyalty.

8434 Columbianus: tundra swan. Swan symbolism has often been seen as a symbol of wisdom and includes awakening the power of self, balance, grace, inner beauty, innocence, self-esteem, seeing into the future, understanding spiritual, evolution, developing intuitive abilities, grace in dealing with others and commitment.

8435 Anser: greylag goose. The goose has a reputation for protection and loyalty. Unity and collaboration. Motherhood/fertility.

8441 Lapponica: bar tailed godwit; known for its audacity.

8589 Stellaris: great bittern. The generic name botaurus. Pliny gave a fanciful derivation from Bos (ox) and Taurus (bull) because the bittern's call resembles the bellowing of a bull. (Stellaris means star.) This may be presented strong in charts of those with connections to the sign of Taurus or Taurus constellation. Known for its ingenuity, patience and spiritual connections with nature. Compassion.

Shadow Side: bitterness, beyond redemption, extreme hatred, coldness or severe temper.

8598 Tetrix: black grouse. Since the late Victorian times, the tails have been popular adornments for hats worn with Highland Dress. Most associated with Glengarry and Balmoral or Tam o' Shanter caps. They continue to be worn by pipers of civilian and military pipe bands.

Keywords: blue collar or military work. Territorial. Self-preservation. Boundaries. Belonging to a close knit, secretive, or exclusive group.

8601 Ciconia: white stork. The Hebrew word for white stork means "merciful or kind". Greek/Roman mythology portray storks as models of parental devotion. Storks also took care of their aging parents in many stories. Storks have little fear of humans if not disturbed and often nest on buildings in Europe. In Germany, the presence of a nest on a house was believed to protect against fires. They were also protected because of the belief that their souls were human. They are believed to bring harmony and fertility to the family.

8965 Citrinella: yellowhammer. An old legend links the yellowhammer to the Devil. Its tongue was supposed to bear a drop of his blood, and the intricate pattern on the eggs was said to carry a concealed, possibly evil, message. These satanic associations sometimes led to the persecution of the bird. The unusual appearance of the eggs also led to "scribble lark", an old name for the bird. Aside from that, there's an old Scottish poem that alludes to the bird and a sexual encounter.

8968 Europaeus: nightjar. Some new world species are called night hawks. Poets have used the nightjar as an indicator of warm summer nights, *"love in the air"*. In Yorkshire, nightjars were said to be the souls of unbaptized children, condemned to wander the world forever.

Keywords: being seriously superstitious; auspicious; uncertainty.

3452 Hawke: "The eye in the sky." Wise like Pallas Athene. She is associated with several birds. She often shape shifts in the form of the hawk. Hawks are known to be wise messengers, commanding attention. The symbolism and stories are too plentiful to list.

Keywords: brilliance, clarity, courage, energy, focus, healing, intensity, intuition, leadership, observation, optimism, power, prophecy, protection, spiritual awareness, strength, unification, vision, and wisdom.

8875 Atthis: kingfisher. The sacred kingfisher, along with other Pacific kingfishers, was venerated by the Polynesians, who believed it had control over the seas and waves.

Keywords: patience, speed, prosperity, agile and quick minded yet shy.

Modern taxonomy also refers to the winds and sea in naming kingfishers after a classical Greek myth. The first pair of mythical-bird Halcyon (kingfishers) were created from a marriage of Alcyone and Ceyx. As gods, they lived the sacrilege of referring to themselves as Zeus and Hera. They died for this, but the other gods, in an act of compassion, made them into birds, thus restoring them to their original seaside habitat. In addition, special "halcyon days" were granted. These are the seven days on either side of the winter solstice when storms shall never again occur for them.

The Halcyon birds' "days" were for caring for the winter-hatched clutch (or brood) but the phrase "Halcyon Days" also refers specifically to an idyllic time in the past, or in general to a peaceful time. The kingfisher's tribe is called the "First One Color."

Keywords: prosperity, fertility, unity, calm weather, spirit guides who improve mental and spiritual intuition.

16421 RoadRunner: bird that darts in front of fast-moving cars; reckless; impulsive; rushed behavior; in a hurry.

2150 Nycitmene: (nocturnal owl) or bat.

In Roman mythology, she was raped or seduced by her father. Out of shame or guilt she fled to the forest and refused to show her face in daylight. Taking pity on her, Minerva transformed her into a nocturnal owl, which, in time became a widespread symbol of the goddess.

She felt that her place as Minerva's sacred bird was embarrassing and became so ashamed of herself that she would not be seen by daylight. The name is also given to a breed of bats.

Keywords: night, bats, the night owl, insomnia, shape shifting, morphing, sorcery, magic, vampires, seeress, flying, birds, low self-esteem, escapism, flight, shame, shadow, jealousy, no voice, darkness, self-doubt, shy, silent partner, image issues, physical abnormalities, restrictions, wisdom, secrets, messenger.

Research Note: *when Corona Virus came out in 2020, this asteroid was prominent in the discovery, release, and control event charts.*

Bird Asteroids in Mythology

8405 Asbolos: he was a seer, or an auger. He was a diviner who read omens in the flight of birds. Auguring/prophecy through the language of birds.

2 Pallas: often took the form of a hawk (shape shifting). She is known for her infinite and invaluable wisdom; birds (hawks, owls) were her sacred messengers.

881 Athene: same as Pallas above.

1924 Horus: depicted with the head of a falcon. "Eye of Horus", all seeing eye. Falconry. Protection.

4543 Phoenix: the great phoenix. Widely recognized as the rising of death, rebirth, and regeneration abilities. The natural cycles. To rise again. Great strength. Shamanism. Mysticism. Transformation. Shifting.

15860 Siran: (Sirin) birds with women heads, lured men to their death (Russia, Greek) similar to the sirens of the sea who lured men to their death by singing.

9106 Yatagarasu: The holy crow or raven with three legs of Japanese mythology. The word Yatagarasu has been translated as "eight-span crow" (i.e. giant crow) and deemed to mean "supreme or perfect divine crow". The number eight in Japanese numerology having the meanings of "many or a multitude", "perfect or supreme", or just "large crow". It is believed the three-legged crow inhabits and represents the Sun. The crow/raven *represents divine guidance and prophecy.*

2307 Garuda: a mythological bird, mount of the god Vishnu, related to kundalini awakening.

4995 Griffin: guard of treasure and priceless possessions (Greek).

3988 Huma: the Huma bird in Iranian mythology is a bird of fortune since its touch, or even sight of its shadow, is said to be auspicious. The Huma bird is said to never come to rest, living its entire life flying invisibly high above the earth, and never touching ground. It is said to be phoenix like, consuming itself in fire every few hundred years, only to rise anew from the ashes.

The Huma bird is said to have both, male and female natures in one body, each nature having one wing and one leg. *Huma is compassionate, and a "'bird of fortune".*

Capturing the Huma is beyond even the wildest imagination but catching a glimpse of it or even a shadow of it is sure to make one happy for the rest of his/her life. **Note**: *it is believed that Huma cannot be caught alive and the person killing a Huma will die in forty days.*

Its true allegory meaning is that when a person's thoughts so evolve that they break all limitation, then he becomes as a king. It is the limitation of language that it can only describe the "most high".

Keywords: reaching a true state of "samadhi" or spiritual ecstasy. Going beyond the veil and reaching new spiritual heights. Good luck. Spiritually ascended. Interdenominational. Astral projection. Shamanic journey. Transformative. Lucky. Awakening. Inner peace. Protection.

Sleep and Dreams

3908 Nyx: goddess of the night. Mother of Hypnos (sleep) and Thanatos (death). It was said she was so powerful that she was feared by Zeus himself.

148780 Altjira: god of dream time. Prophetic dreams. Supernatural; fantasy. Planets in aspect patterns with Altjira describe what you encounter in the world of visions and dreams; what impact dreams have. Lucid dreaming.

1298 Nocturna: belonging to the night.

14827 Hypnos: god of sleep. Lucid dreams if close to Neptune, Jupiter, or Moon.

12746 Yumeginga: dream galaxy. Yume means "dream" and ginga means "galaxy".

Keywords: a fantasy world; being connected to the galaxy (cosmos) through dreams; idealized location; hope; escapism.

H56 White Moon Selene: Moon goddess. (This is the hypothetical point, not the asteroid.) The purest and brightest moonlight that bathes the spirit in Divine Healing white light. Protection. The brightest, purest essence showing the path of light, during the darkest of times.

Keywords: truth, purity, healing, stepping into higher consciousness, authentic intentions, removing blockages through healing arts. Using Selene(a) brings blessings, integrity, authenticity, and protective wards against negative energies.

580 Selene: Moon goddess (asteroid) same as Selene(a) above.

10412 Tsukuyomi: Moon god; light of night.

200025 Cloudgate: dream cloud, memory gate.

5710 Silentium: silence, quiet, stillness, calm.

4197 Morpheus: god of dreams. Use with Neptune/Moon and Jupiter.

341520 Mors-Somnus: gods of sleep and death (death in sleep).

Note: transit may show in death charts of persons who passed away in sleep.

3258 Somnium: dreams; shadow side, could be insomnia/trouble sleeping. Look at transits to see if it is hitting a hotspot in your chart when having sleep issues.

54362 Restitutum: Latin term for "something that has been replaced or restored to its former place". This minor planet was originally lost soon after discovery, then found again.

Keywords: resting place; finding something lost; waking up feeling restored and refreshed. Feeling revived; renewed; restorative properties. Nothing or anyone is truly lost, it just hasn't been found yet.

94 Aurora: Sleeping Beauty; hard time waking from sleep/dreams.

15438 Joegotobed: "Joe go to bed"; bed time, staying up too late.

1257 Mora: (Mare) in Slavic folklore. A malicious entity that rides on people's chests while they sleep, bringing on bad dreams. "Nightmare" or "to harm". Haunt. Possible derivative of Moros (death). Mares included witches who took on the form of animals when their spirits went out and about while they were in trance. It is a common belief that mora enters the room through the keyhole, sits on the chest of the sleepers and tries to strangle them, "to torture", "to bother", "to strangle,", "to tire","to kill", "tiredness".

Keywords: haunt, nightmares, cause harm, shape shift, sleep paralysis. Scared to death. Frightful. Psychic attack. Dark sorcery and curses.

Note: *not to be confused with "Moira", the Greek Fates.*

16974 Iphthime: was Penelope's sister, who appears to her in a dream and comforts her as she is grieving. Messages delivered via dreams; communicating with loved ones who are deceased; encouragement and reassurance from the spirit world.

432 Pythia: famous Oracle of Delphi who breathed deeply and inhaled the fumes of decaying snakes to enter a trance-like state to prophecy. She is *very* prominent in prophetic/lucid dreaming.

Note: *following her transits, will shine a light into your sleeping/dream state when she hits your natal Moon, Neptune, or Jupiter.*

7399 Somme: means "tranquility" in Celtic. It could also be attributed to sleeping, rest, peace, or meditation.

Dream Lore
Switzerland:

According to the beliefs of the people and the shepherds who live in the wild mountainous region surrounding the Waldstätter Lake in Switzerland, there is a cave in a cliff there where the three redeemers, called the Three Tells, are sleeping. Dressed in ancient costume, they will arise, come forth, and rescue their fatherland when the need arises. Only the very lucky have succeeded in finding the entrance to the cave.

A shepherd boy told the following story to a traveler: His father, looking for a lost goat among the cliffs, came upon this cave and entered it. As soon as he recognized the three sleeping men as the Three Tells, one of them rose up and asked: "What time is it on Earth?" The frightened shepherd answered "It is high noon." The man replied: "It is not yet time for us to come." and went back to sleep. The father returned with his companions to awaken the Tells for the good of the threatened fatherland, and although he looked repeatedly, he never again found the cave.

Source: Jacob and Wilhelm Grimm, Deutsche Sagen (1816/1818), no. 298. --https://www.pitt.edu/~dash/sleep.html

Justice and Law

3528 Council Man: politician.
13 Egeria: she imparted laws and rituals pertaining to Ancient Roman religion. Wisdom and prophecy.
249521 Truth: finding and telling the truth.
9133 D'Arrest: arrested; caught; captured; use in crime charts.
160 Una: the personification of the "true church". She travels with the Red Cross Knight (England) whom she has recruited to save her parents' castle from a dragon. She also defeats Duessa, who represents the "false" Catholic church and the reason Mary, Queen of Scots was beheaded. Una is representative of the journey for truth.
Keywords: truth; constantly in search of truths; honorable in action.
7207 Hammurabi: king of Babylon; Hammurabi code "an eye for an eye, tooth for a tooth"; code of laws and ethics, and the punishments to be enforced.
3279 Solon: Greek lawmaker. He is remembered particularly for his efforts to legislate against political, economic and moral decline in Archaic Athens.
Keywords: politics; politician; justice system; social justice; non-traditionalist; open minded to change.
679 Pax: Roman goddess of peace.
269 Justitia: goddess of justice.
38083 Rhadhamanthus: judges and punisher of the unworthy souls in the underworld; known for few legislative (laws).
5 Astraea: she was the virgin goddess of innocence and purity, and is always associated with the Greek goddess of justice. In the Tarot, the 8th card, Justice, with a figure of Justitia, can thus be considered related to the figure of Astraea on historical iconographic grounds (Wiki).
15 Eunomia: goddess of law and legislation; her name can be translated as "good order".
24 Themis: goddess of justice; divine law and order.
93 Minerva: Roman goddess of wisdom, war, justice, law and victory. She was also the patron of the arts, trade, and strategy. She is the Roman version of Pallas/Athene.
5731 and H42 Zeus: the god of law and social order; enforced the cosmic laws that governed them. Strategic, ruthless yet wise. He was appalled by human sacrifices and decided to wipe out mankind and flooded the world with the help of his brother Poseidon. He was also known

as a notorious womanizer with infidelities too long to list. Rules for thee, but not for me. He is associated with the planet Jupiter.

474 Prudentia: to be prudent, judicious or wise.

9 Metis: prudence and wisdom; she was known as the "wise counsellor".

37 Fides: fruthful; honest; trustworthy.

58 Concordia: peacekeeper, peaceful, seeking peace agreements.

490 Veritas: truth, truthfulness. Veritas was a Roman goddess often appearing naked with a mirror; "the naked truth".

1464 Armisticia: peace-making, effective negotiator.

6630 Skepticus: skeptical, uncertain, doubtful, guarded judgement.

99 Dike: goddess of justice, and the spirit of moral order, and fair judgement.

14 Irene: goddess of peace and the season of spring. She was one of the three Horai (Hope) deities of the seasons and keepers of the gates of heaven. Her sisters were Eunomia (Good order) and Dike (Justice).

252 Clementina: goddess of clemency, leniency, mercy, forgiveness, penance, redemption, absolution and salvation.

3811 Karma: cosmic law and order.

Good to follow for transits.

20000 Varuna: Vedic ruler of the worlds, the ordained and enforcer of law; upholder of the world order. Supreme god capable of controlling and dispensing justice.

134 Sophrosyne: temperance, moderation, prudence, purity, and self-control. Honesty. Good judgement of character.

609 Fulvia: she was known as the wife to Mark Antony. She's the ideal "politicians' wife". Politics and business. Supportive. Reputable. Intelligent. Behind the scenes support. Loyal. Respected advice.

52963 Vercingetorix: was a king of the Arverni and military leader of the Celtic people against the Roman invasion. He raised an army of the poor and made alliances with other tribes. He beat Julius Caesar's forces at the Battle of Gergovia but surrendered during the battle of Alesia, presumably because of superstitions related to the lunar eclipse, and to save as many of his men as possible, he gave himself to the Romans. Name translates as "great warrior king".

Keywords: very superstitious. Self-sacrificing. Leader. Respected. Loyal. He was fighting against the elite on behalf of the poor village people who stood no chance on their own. He was resourceful. Kind. Took care of the underdog. Protective. Stood against injustices and unfairness.

Asian

10547 Yosakoi: means "come at night" and is a popular Japanese folk song about the forbidden love between a monk and a girl. Song talks of a monk in love! Shockingly, a unique case of a monk who could not take it any more for a woman that he had loved. So, he had to look for a way of expressing his love for her. He resorted to buying a hair ornament for her. The monk used to meet his love at night. It's also a very popular dance that combines Japanese traditional and new age techniques together. The duality at play here should not be ignored. Possibly may show an "odd" couple in synastry charts. *Throwing away everything to surrender to true love. Overcoming the odds. Meeting halfway. A combination of Saturn (tradition) with a twist of Uranus (new age).*

10604 Susanoo: Japanese god of heroes and younger brother of the goddess Amaterasu. He is also the powerful storm god of summer and seas.

10613 Kushinadahime: the mythical empress of the god Susanoo who was offered as a sacrifice to the giant snake Yamata-no-orochi but was saved by Susanoo (above).

10768 Sarutahiko: a Japanese Shinto deity and guardian of Earth; "great bright god"; "greatly virtuous god"; symbol of strength and guidance; standing between Heaven and Earth, being one with the Universe, and so achieving peace with the world. Namaste.

10385 Amaterasu: Sun goddess/deity; "shining in heaven"; ruler of the high plains in heaven.

10804 Amenouzume: the goddess of dawn, mirth and sensual revelry. She performed a dance in front of a cave to coax the Sun goddess Amaterasu back outside and restore the light to earth. She overturned a tub near the entrance of the cave where the Sun was hiding, and began to dance on it, tearing off her clothing in front of the other deities. They considered this so comical that they laughed heartily at the sight. She is known as "the great persuader". If strongly aspected with Venus or Mercury, the person could be a natural performer or dancer.

10831 Takamagahara: heaven; bridge to heaven. Spiritually connected to a higher realm.

10412 Tsukuyom: Moon god.

1047 Geisha: "art person"; a Japanese hostess trained to entertain men with conversation, dance, and song. Like the Greek muses. Performer. Hostess. Traditionalist.

10888 Yamatano-orochi: is a giant snake dragon appearing in Japanese ancient mythology. The snake had eight heads and eight tails, and was long enough to cover eight valleys and eight peaks. It was defeated by the god Susanoo. (Notice the triple eights in the asteroid number and the fact this creature has eight heads.)

10162 Issunboushi: the extraordinarily small character Issunboushi- Issun means "about three cm" in old Japanese; was the hero of many old Japanese tales. Born the size of a bean, he defeated ogres, succeeded in a stratagem that got him a beautiful bride, and shook a mallet that instantly transformed him into a normal young man.

Keywords: good things in small packages; don't discount the underdog; don't judge a book by the cover. Bravery. Overcoming physical limitations.

10209 Izanaki: according to the Japanese myth, Izanaki-no-mikoto is the god who descended to the island Onogoro with the goddess Izanami and created the land there, including the island of Awaji.

48482 Oruki: Japanese, meaning "the importance of one's presence and reassurance of unflagging support".

10227 Izanami: Izanami-no-mikoto is the mythical goddess who descended to the island Onogoro with the god Izanaki and various other gods. After her death she was also called Yomotsu-ookami in the land of the dead.

10223 Zashikiwarashi: taking the form of a child with bobbed hair, Zashikiwarashi is a traditional spirit of the people of the Tohoku district. It haunts the Japanese-style rooms of old families. It is said that a family would be wealthy while the spirit lives and become poor when it leaves.

162173 Ryugu: means "Dragon Palace Castle". In Japanese folklore it is the undersea palace of Ryūjin, the dragon Kami of the sea. Depending on the version of the legend, it is built from red and white coral, or from solid crystal. The inhabitants of the palace were Ryūjin's families and servants, who were denizens of the sea. In some legends, on each of the four sides of the palace it is a different season, and one day in the palace is equal to a century outside its boundaries.

5072 Hioki: in Japanese, the word means "place where picturesque sun sets.". Sun. Positive outlook. Daytime optimistic. Bright and clear. Dynamic. Shining brightly.

9110 Choukai: possible meanings: listen; headstrong; naughty; careful inquiry; unravel notes; key; explanation; understanding; untie; undo; solve; answer; cancel; absolve.

120 Kobe: translates to "god door", gateway to heaven; also, prime beef and a Japanese city. Possible meanings: high quality; luxury; premier; top of the line; reach the top.

25143 Itokawa: I've seen different meanings and just keep coming back to "rocket scientist". Possibly, he could represent a blockage, or an uphill battle, being stubborn to not quit and taking the long road to success.

9106 Yatagarasu: the holy crow, or raven with three legs of Japanese mythology. The word Yatagarasu has been translated as "eight-span crow" (i.e. giant crow) and deemed to mean "supreme or perfect divine crow". The number eight in Japanese numerology having the meanings of "many or a multitude", or "perfect or supreme", or just "large crow". It is believed the three-legged crow inhabits and represents the Sun. The crow/raven *represents divine guidance and prophecy.*

11064 Dogen: the founding father of Japanese Soto Zen. Was a Japanese Zen Buddhist monk, writer, poet, and philosopher. He believed, when practitioners of Zen attain Daigo, they have risen above the discrimination between delusion and enlightenment. According to the traditional interpretation, uji "means time itself is being, and all being is time." Dōgen writes that "whole-being is the Buddha-nature" and that even inanimate objects (rocks, sand, water) are an expression of Buddha-nature. He rejected any view that saw Buddha-nature as a permanent, substantial inner self, or ground. Dōgen describes Buddha-nature as "vast emptiness", "the world of becoming", and writes that "impermanence is in itself Buddha-nature."

Keywords: exist. Be. Have time. Exist as one with nature. To be is to be time itself.

150 Nuwa: the mother goddess in Chinese mythology. She is credited with creating mankind and repairing the Pillar of Heaven.

Keywords: create; repair; rebuild; nourish; manifest; bridge between worlds; protection; remodeling; to make new again; peace; tranquility; paradise found; reinvigorate; loving touches; comfort; going on vacation.

21390 Shindo: a term for Korean Shamanism. In the new age movement, it's used to say, "intense energy". It's also a term used to describe seismic activity, which is essentially "intense energy shifts".

Keywords: energy healers, reiki, meditation points, past life regression sessions; feeling shifts in earth's frequency; ritual work; deep shadow work.

52500 Kanata: Japanese for "far away" or "beyond", "the distance".

Keywords: this could reflect where we are willing to "go the distance" and put in the extra effort. Depending on house placement, for example in 10th house career and success driven. 7th house relationship/partnership. 6th house being of service, healing. 1st house going the distance to better yourself. 2nd house going the distance for stability. Daydreaming; losing track of time; futuristic outlook.

Shadow Side: reaching for something that is too far away and unrealistic to grab. Setting the bar too high.

Time

In history, Saturn is the timekeeper that measures out the story of man. As timekeeper, it measures out birth and death. It is the activator of beginnings and endings. Lord of Karma. A colleague and I are working on a theory, about people who have natal Saturn in retrograde, experience "time" differently than those with a direct Saturn. For example, a person with a retrograde Saturn, may have no "time awareness" or literally lose track of times and dates more frequently than those with a direct Saturn. Additionally, a person with a stationary Saturn (not moving) could feel stuck in a karmic loop, or have issues keeping boundaries, especially if this Saturn squares the Nodes. It may feel as if they are in quicksand and may manifest as they try to move faster than others, for fear of sinking.

H43 Kronos (Saturn) : lord of karma/time (hypothetical point).

3811 Karma : keeper of time/life debts.

4227 Kaali : goddess of time/death.

923 Herluga: timekeeper, clock; from French word "horloge", hourglass of life. Look at aspects with Saturn, the cosmic timekeeper. Activations of beginning and endings. Transits with vertex/antivertex = fated events. Alternate name for a Japanese Fandom character = Cheerful Vampire.

420356 Praamzius: ruler of time/fate.

3325 TARDIS: Time and Relative Dimension in Space (time machine).

15332 CERN: associated with time travel/time portals/time waves.

6735 Madhatter: stuck in an eternal tea party in the belief that the hatter has murdered time, and it is permanently 6 o'clock.

Ever felt stuck in a perpetual loop replaying the same patterns over and over again?

730 Athanasia: Greek for "immortality." Infinite. Lasting forever. Eternal. Timeless. Unending existence. Everlasting.

Mystery of Time

According to great scientists such as Albert Einstein, time is not as stable as most of us think.

As humans, we're adjusted to time and our evolution has established tricks that allow our conscious minds to deal with it, but in reality, it is a slippery concept.

Time slips occur when a current time (now) interlaces with a previous time (then) and can be experienced by the person from the more recent time.

However, the event is usually unnoticed by the people from the earlier time.

What is the evidence for this phenomenon?

In fact, it is so common that we've even built it into the English language.

When a time slip occurs, people in both realities can experience the alternative reality simultaneously.

Still, according to most accounts, this usually lasts for only a few seconds and the human brain does its best to filter out these anomalies.

This has given rise to expressions such as "I could have sworn that I've just seen" or "my eyes must be playing tricks on me" or even "you won't believe what I just saw".

Over the years people have claimed that they've seen old airplanes parked in fields that were once airports or roman soldiers marching down their road.

In almost all cases the person experiencing the time slip blinks, looks again and is startled to find that whatever they saw has now vanished.

However, photography has captured these anomalies from the time that the camera was first invented.

In fact, the longer exposure times of early cameras have revealed more than the modern "instant" versions do but there are still oddities such as the image captured on Google Earth that clearly shows a World War Two bomber flying over Britain.

Not every time slip is brief and there have been occasions when people have entered a room and been startled to find that they are in a completely different timeline.

Alice in Wonderland

Alice in Wonderland has a recurring metaphor: Alice going down the rabbit hole is a philosopher's quest for true knowledge. The spiritual quest of wisdom and understanding. The same can be said about learning astrology.

Wonderland is a place of madness. "We're all mad here," states the Cheshire cat.

Through the eyes of society, one who questions, even and perhaps especially the seemingly basic things, may be labelled "mad".

The Moon is the "marker of time" (Saturn's creation) and therefore gives us the illusion of time.

For example, the white rabbit and his pocket watch in Alice and Wonderland are all symbols for the Moon, Saturn, and the goddess (Alice) as "Wonderland" is the illusion of existence. Alice being the "goddess archetype" is trapped by time in the Saturn- Moon matrix.

291 Alice: your inner child; represents where you step out into the world on your own. The way you "grow up" or become an adult. Alice is you! She questions her appearance, being "too big or too small". She doesn't understand the changes her body is making in puberty. She doesn't understand why the things she was taught are all wrong. Curiosity.

453 Tea: it's the trigger to take the first step away from the crowd and find yourself. It's also the "gossip" or the "situation" that is exposed to push you to learn more, discover more, it makes you ask questions.

17518 Red Queen: represents the suppression of truth to keep the masses asleep. Mind control. Brainwashing. Control through fear tactics. Followers. Where one follows the crowd and loses individual identity.

6735 Madhatter: stuck in an eternal tea party believing that the hatter has murdered time, and it is permanently 6 o'clock.

Ever felt stuck in a perpetual loop replaying the same patterns repeatedly? Going "mad", losing one's head. Controlled chaos. Matrix. Going in circles with no defined outcome with no understanding of why you are going in circles to begin with? Repetitive. Infinite. Making the same mistakes over and over. Never to make a definite choice. In flux.

17942 White Rabbit: the teacher; the philosopher, leading the student down the rabbit hole of curiosity. White Rabbit symbolizes the curiosity and sparks the transformation of "awakening". Wise teacher. Questioning reality as one knows it.

6736 Marchare: may be just slightly on the eccentric side, a little "loopy," and somewhat unconventional in their behavior. They can also be unpredictable; one moment they are sane, the next as "mad as March hares".

17746 Haigha: the marchare in Alice in Wonderland. Same as above.

6042 Chessirecat: appears and disappears with an infamous grin. The elusive truth. The truth isn't always transparent, one must learn how to discern for themselves.

17681 Tweedledum and 9387 Tweedledee: Tweedle Dee and Tweedle Dum tell Alice the tale of the Curious Oysters, which is about how curiosity can lead to terrible consequences. This shows how adults often use stories to control children with fear, and to destroy children's sense of imagination and curiosity by telling them to quit asking questions and grow up. *"Tweedle Dee and Tweedle Dum symbolize parents who are trying to keep Alice's imagination in check." ~ Internet source.*

8889 Mockturtle: "mock" is fake; not real. He wants to be "real" but realizes he doesn't really "exist" in the physical form. He's always crying and sobbing because he just wants to be a real turtle. This may be the place one pretends to be something or someone they are not just to fit in. The fakeness of society's superficial standards of what is considered "normal". Not loving oneself for who they really are. Insecurities.

17612 WhiteKnight: the White Knight saves Alice from his opponent. He repeatedly falls off his horse and lands on his head, he entertains Alice with his ideas of quirky inventions.

Keywords: the good guy, hero, savior, comedic relief, jokester, witty, humble, friend, protector, clumsy.

6136 Gryphon: the gryphon had an eagle's head, front half with wings and talons, and the back of a lion's legs and tail. Gryphon appears to be somewhat overbearing and dismissive of the obsessions and dismays of the other characters.

Keywords: indifferent; unphased. Bully. Making someone uncomfortable. Abrasive, shrewd personality. Ability to push someone out of their comfort zone. Where we are forced to face reality. The "tough love" approach. Hurting feelings to help move along the process of facing buried emotions. Removing "rose colored glasses". The tough professor pushing boundaries because they see truths and potential. Finding one's courage and honor.

Weather and Natural Disasters

1980 Tezcatlipoca: god of night winds and hurricanes.

1915 Quetzalcoatl: god of wind; hurricanes.

38628 Huya: (TNO) rain god of the Wayuu people of Venezuela and Colombia. It has very Neptunian qualities. And in my experience, it depicts survival. How hard will you fight? In what way? To save your life and those you love in hard times? Sort of like the corny marriage vows "in sickness and in health" etc. How far are you willing to hang in there and fight? (Not the violent kind, the emotional watery Neptune fight.) Huya can also depict how we "make it rain". For those who know pop culture, this is in reference to how we build a fortune or build our empire. Our influence or affluence as well. How/what is your gift to manifest for the world? Slippery slopes? Be careful what you wish for? When the people wished for rain, did they not think ahead and ask for how much or request moderation? Do you know your limits? Flooding, or floating? Balance.

4341 Poseidon: god of the sea and earthquakes.

42355 Typhon: winged monster (dragon like) who caused huge storms and massive destruction. Typhoons; earthquakes; volcanoes; natural weather disasters.

3200 Phaethon: wildfires; fiery mass destruction.

79360 Sila Nunam: Sila is the Inuit god of the sky, weather, and life force. Nunam is the Earth goddess.

37655 Illapa: very important thunder or weather god of the Incas. He had the power to make rain, hail and thunder; he also mastered clouds. They prayed to Illapa for rain and protection from drought.

12152 Aratus: weather forecasts and phenomenon; Greek poet known for his poem called "Phenomena". He followed the constellations and correlated those with certain weather events. He also published "forecasts". The crater Aratus on the Moon is named after him.

Keywords: weather phenomenon; anomalies; forecasts and predictions.

20002 Tillysmith: British girl who, by recognizing the signs of a tsunami, saved many lives on the island of Phuket, December 26, 2004.

5352 Fujita: original F scale for tornado warning system, i.e. EF4 tornado.

5109 Robert Miller: first meteorologist to issue a tornado forecast.

2629 Rudra: roaring storm god; associated with wind, storms and hunt. Terror; most frightening.

1170 Siva: (Shiva) destroyer god of the universe to re-create it. Hindus believe his powers of destruction and recreation are used to destroy the illusions and imperfections of this world, paving the way for powerful, transformational change.

20000 Varuna: god of oceans/water.

427 Galene: goddess of calm seas. Her name means "calm weather" or calm/tranquility. *Note: similar to achieving the state of Samadhi through meditation.*

99942 Apophis: lord of chaos, enemy of the Sun; snakes and watery underworld darkness. Destruction.

10604 Susanoo: Japanese powerful storm god of summer and seas.

12923 Zephyr: was the west wind god and bringer of light spring and early-summer breezes.

Keywords: weather; winds, west, spring; gentle calm winds; breezes breath of fresh air.

2212 Hephaistos: god of volcanoes and fire.

4464 Vulcano: volcanoes; fire; lava/land destruction.

2202 Pele: Hawaiian volcano goddess.

14764 Kilauea: Hawaiian volcano.

13897 Vesuvius: Italian volcano.

85047 Krakatoa: (My favorite volcano story.) Shockwave heard around the world.

85095 Hekla: Iceland's most active volcano. Europeans called the volcano the "Gateway to Hell" or "Hell's Chimney." Hekla is also the word for a short, hooded cloak.

19521 Chaos: destruction; havoc.

H41 Hades: underworld; darkness; destruction.

11885 Summanus: was the Etruscan or Roman deity responsible for nocturnal lightning and thunder. Name possibly means "the greatest of manes". The "manes" were thought to represent souls of deceased loved ones.

Keywords: darkness, nighttime thunderstorms; lightening strike; gloomy; nocturnal; lost souls of the night; cynical outlook.

217 Eudora: Greek Hyad of the Haydes. Name translates to "the rainy one", sisterhood of nymphs who bring rain. Also called the "rain stars". The Haydes star cluster is located at 5-6 Gemini, situated on the face of the bull in the Taurus constellation. Possible star seed origin asteroid.

2020 Ukko: supreme Finnish god. God of sky, weather, harvest, lightning and thunder. His weapon was a hammer and he is similar to Thor and Zeus.

136472 MakeMake: creator god of the indigenous people of Easter Island. MakeMake is not an asteroid. It is the third largest dwarf planet that takes 310 years to orbit the sun. It is prominent in ecological disaster charts.

Keywords: with destruction comes creation; severe weather events; volcanic eruptions; tsunami threats; threats of disease from foreign lands; population reduction events.

5731 and H42 Zeus: god of thunder/sky, (asteroid Zeus/hypothetical point Zeus).

1916 Boreas: god the cold north wind and bringer of cold winter air. Boreas is depicted as being very strong, with a violent temper. He was closely associated with horses and was said to have fathered twelve colts after taking the form of a stallion.

Keywords: blizzards, cold fronts, strong winds; winter; spirit horse.

133 Cyrene: "Sovereign Queen" and was a fierce huntress; the girl lion killer. When a lion attacked her father's sheep, Cyrene wrestled with the lion. Apollo, who was present, immediately fell in love with her.

Keywords: protector, hunter/huntress, not conforming to gender specific stereotypes, inner and physical strength; cannot be controlled, not ruled by anyone or anything, pure power. Object of obsession and desires; unique qualities; stand out in the crowd.

4250 Perun: Slavic god of thunder and lightning. His other attributes were fire, mountains, wind, rain, and storms. The oak tree; the eagle (spirit). He is strongly attributed to making weapons with stone and metal. Norse equivalent to Thor.

Keywords: weapons and weather events.

3905 Doppler: weather radars used to predict storms and patterns.

H46 Vulkanus and H55 Vulcan: volcano; fire (hypothetical points).

29198 Weather

4220 Flood

12182 Storm

221019 Raine

3742 Sunshine

7536 Fahrenheit: temperatures.

4169 Celsius: temperatures.

854 Frostia: frozen; cold; blizzard, frost, snow, and ice.

Moon

16912 Rhiannon: Celtic Moon goddess.

4047 Chang'E: Chinese Moon goddess and immortality. She is also associated with space travel.

On the full Moon night of the eighth lunar month, an open-air altar is set up facing the Moon for the worship of Chang'e. New pastries are put on the altar for her to bless. She is said to endow her worshippers with beauty.

Side note: *Chang'e is the name of the Chinese vessel that recently landed on the dark side of the Moon.*

3271 Ul: a lunar deity in Vanuatu. Moon god.

H56 White Moon Selene(a) and Asteriod Selene 580: the purest and brightest moonlight that bathes the spirit in Divine healing white light. Protection. The brightest, purest essence showing the path of light, during the darkest of times.

Keywords: truth, purity, healing, stepping into higher consciousness, authentic intentions, removing blockages through healing arts. Using Selene(a) brings blessings, integrity, authenticity, and protective wards against negative energies.

10412 Tsukuyomi: Moon god; light of night.

7805 Moons

270 Anahita: a river goddess who was also goddess of Venus and the Moon. Her name means "pure" or "immaculate one" as she represented the cleansing and fertilizing flow of the cosmos.

105 Artemis: the Greek goddess of the hunt, nature, and birth. This maiden goddess is symbolized by the crescent Moon.

1958 Chandra: Hindu lord of the Moon.

78 Diana: Goddess of the hunt and wild animals. She later took over from Luna as the Roman goddess of the Moon, responsible for fertility and childbirth.

395 Delia: alternative name for the Greek goddess Artemis (Diana).

1067 Lunaria: means moonlight. It's a species of flowering plants commonly called "honesty".

100 Hekate: triple Moon goddess, deeply associated with the waning and dark moons. She is depicted as a haunting crone at the crossroads with her two large hounds, carrying a torch, symbolic of her great wisdom.

7088 Ishtar: some myths say she is the daughter of the Moon, others the mother.

42 Isis: powerful and widely worshipped goddess, was not only a Moon deity, but a goddess of the Sun as well.

21670 Kuan: Kuan Yin; a Buddhist goddess. Modern feminist Pagans believe she far pre-dates Buddhist origins. She was a goddess of the Moon, compassion, and healing.

146 Lucina: goddess of light with both solar and lunar attributes. She was Christianized as St. Lucia, a saint still honored at Yule in many parts of Europe.

85 Io: This is an asteroid, but Io is also the name of one of Jupiter's moons. She was one of the mortal lovers of Zeus. Zeus noticed Io, a mortal woman, and lusted after her. She initially rejected Zeus' advances, until her father threw her out of his house on the advice of oracles. According to some stories, Zeus then turned Io into a heifer to hide her from his wife. Pitying the unfortunate girl, Gaia, the goddess of the earth, created the violet. The various colors of the violet (red, purple, white) changed on account of Io's life, red for the blushing maiden, purple for the cow, white for the stars. The ancients connected Io with the Moon and the "horned virgin".

17936 Nilus: god of the Nile river.

Keywords: Water-Neptune-Moon = depths and emotions. The river runs deep. It also twists and turns, so thoughts could be scattered if this asteroid is conjunct Neptune. With it the Moon offers insight with its guiding light.

84921 Morkoláb: Hungarian mythical animal that eats the Sun or Moon during an eclipse. This object was discovered during a total lunar eclipse. Also associated with the underworld. *Look at the transits during eclipses.*

Recommend using alongside:

148780 Altjira: god of dreamtime; prophetic/lucid dreams.

Business and Fortune:

1981 Midas: everything he touched turned to gold.
33154 Talent: skill, gift, ability, expertise.
307 Nike: goddess of victory.
39382 Opportunity: chance, favorable moment.
19 Fortuna: fortunate; fortune.
258 Tyche: fortune, luck, fate *(best used for transits)*.
151 Abundantia: abundance, overflowing riches, plentiful.
147 Protogenia: goddess of success in business.
7292 Prosperin: to prosper, thrive.
5731 Zeus: well planned efforts, drive for success, leadership, creativity.
10054 Solomin: wisdom and wealth; logic and strategic.
4416 Ramses: Ramses the Great, most powerful pharaoh; respected leader, admired, accomplished. Great success.
58534 Logos: logic, integrity, skillful salesmen, persuasiveness; stats; logistics; details.
50000 Quaoar: creation, new ideas, innovation, new perspectives, pioneers, inventors, entrepreneurs.
21409 Forbes: fortune, investment, riches.
22562 Wage: income, salary.
4955 Gold
5325 Silver
2025 Nortia: Etruscan goddess of fortune.
1838 Ursa: means "bear". The bear symbolism is vast. The Big Dipper and Little Dipper constellations are called "Ursa Major" and "Ursa Minor". The bear symbolizes strength and is widely respected in native cultures as a shamanic spirit of protection, courage and wisdom. *It should be looked at for transits during a "bear market" in stock exchange.*
14927 Satoshi: name used by the unknown person or people who developed bitcoin.
Keywords: bitcoin; digital/crypto currency; blockchain technology; computer science; money market or manager; mystery identity.
139 Juewa: Chinese for "Star of China's Fortune".
Keywords: fortune, prosperity, luck.
11421 Cardano: Gerolamo Cardano. A Renaissance mathematician, physician, biologist, physicist, chemist, astrologer, astronomer, philoso-

pher, writer, and gambler. He was one of the most influential mathematicians of the Renaissance and was one of the key figures in the foundation of probability, and the earliest introducer of the binomial coefficients and the binomial theorem in the western world. He wrote more than two hundred works on science.

He is a little bit of everything. But I want to bring up the modern-day connection to crypto currency. Cardano is a decentralized public blockchain and cryptocurrency project and is fully open source. Cardano is the driving force behind blockchain- developing a smart contract platform which seeks to deliver more advanced features than any protocol previously developed. It is the first blockchain platform to evolve out of a scientific philosophy and a research-first driven approach.

Keywords: cryptocurrency, technology, blockchain, futuristic, money markets, stock markets; money brokerage; gambler, well educated; high intellect; investments. Statistics and mathematical perspectives. It would be noteworthy to observe any Uranus and Mercury aspects to this asteroid.

Death:

Disclaimer: This list is not literally a "death list" and should not be studied in fear. Everyone has these asteroids in their chart. You can NOT use this list to determine a literal death.

14502 Morden: death; murder.

273 Atropos: fate who chose the mechanism of death and ended the life of mortals.

341520 Mors Somnus: god of death (Mors) and sleep (Somnus). Dying in one's sleep; *check transits for location if having surgery with anesthesia.*

71 Niobe: painful mother who loses all her children; murdered children or family; family annihilators; murder/suicide.

171 Ophelia: insanity; death by drowning.

1912 Anubis: deity of funerals and death.

1923 Osiris: god of the dead.

1863 Antinous: deified after death in Egypt. The local priesthood immediately deified Antinous by identifying him with Osiris due to the manner of his death. In keeping with Egyptian custom, Antinous' body was embalmed and mummified by priests, a lengthy process which might explain why Hadrian remained in Egypt until spring. Inscriptions indicate that Antinous was seen primarily as a benevolent deity, who could be turned to aid his worshippers. He was also seen as a *conqueror of death*, with his name and image often being included in coffins.

Keywords: cult activity. Because of the way he was deified to start a cult following; creating a new following; branching out to start a new progressive movement. Blood sacrifices. Unconventional views.

2546 Libitina: goddess of funerals and burials (death). When found on the IC, a person may be exposed to deaths at an early age. They may experience life as "death" mentality.

208 Lacrimosa: tearful, sorrows, from the Catholic Church mass prayer: Full of tears will be that day when from the ashes shall arise.

Keywords: sorrow, tearful, tragedy, mournful, empathy, emotional.

69 Hesperia: to bring an end, peacefully ride away, connected to the Pleiades, final resting place, golden light western sunsets; may possibly indicate assisted end of life deaths.

4227 Kaali: goddess of death, time, and endings.

1170 Siva: destroyer god.

H41 Hades: god of underworld, (home of the dead).
This is a hypothetical point, not an asteroid.
2254 Requiem: funeral mass for the dead; burial rituals.
287 Nephthys: presided over funerals.
5381 Sekhmet: "Before Whom Evil Trembles", "Mistress of Dread", "Lady of Slaughter", and "She Who Mauls".
42 Isis: assists the dead in the afterlife, protector of the dead souls.
3989 Odin: Norse god of wisdom, death, divination, and magic.
90482 Orcus: death and underworld; punisher of broken oaths.
699 Hela: Norse goddess of the dead. Realm of "hell".
949 Hel: Same as above (Hela).
10831 Takamagahara: dwelling place of the heavenly gods; heaven.
3276: Porta Coeli: Heaven's Gate.
8100 Nobeyama: "Yama" is the god of death (Vedic).
638 Moira: Fate.
1808 Bellerophon: fatal crashes; crippled.
4451 Grieve: mourning; grief; sorrow.
248 Lameia: losing a child; grief; murder; "sucks life from" ghosts, or spirits of the dead who had not had a proper funeral rite and so could not lie at rest; sucked the souls of children.
117 Lomia: same as Lameia above.
18 Melpomene: grief; mourning, great sadness, depression.
877 Walkure: in Norse mythology, a Valkyrie is one in a group of female figures who decide which soldiers die in battle and which live.
15810 Arawn: the Celtic god of the dead, war, revenge, and terror within the Welsh mythology. He reigns supreme as the ruler of the spiritual realm of Annwn.
28978 Ixion: murder; lawless; rebellion; impulsive; mass violence.
466 Tisiphone: one of the three Furies; she is the one who punished crimes of murder: parricide, fratricide, and homicide.
911 Agamemnon: mass casualties.
430 Hybris: was a spirit demon or goddess of insolence, violence, and outrageous behavior. Irrational, selfish. Transit may show in drunk driving accidents.
9305 Hazard: car/transportation accidents.
83982 Crantor: sudden unexpected death *(esp. if transit is activating Mars)*.
666 Desdemona: her name means "ill fated".
Keywords: sad, depressed, mournful, feeling victimized. The numer-

ology of this asteroid is number 666. Shows up in tragedies.

7724 Moroso: hopelessness; losing hope; depression; doom and gloom; defaulting; delinquent; at fault.

3849 Incidentia: incident or noteworthy events and occurrences. Situation or experience at a particular place and time that will be remembered. *Note: in notable event charts, look for where this asteroid is transitioning.*

Additional explanations:

Melpomene shows up in grief charts by transit when someone "tragically" lost a loved one. *Notably, if it conjuncts one of these others with Moon, Mars, Neptune, and/or Saturn.*

The Fates should all be considered. Atropos is here because she is the "end".

Isis: resurrects her slain husband by piecing him back together. She was believed to help the dead enter the afterlife. She is said to have power over "fate" itself, and she resided over funerary practices and rituals.

Odin: Odin oversees Valhalla, (Hall of the Chosen Dead) where he receives half of those who die in battle. Military deaths.

Orcus: "Pluto's twin"; god of the land of the dead. The name "Orcus" seems to have been given to his evil and punishing side, as the god who tormented evildoers in the afterlife. Like the name Hades (or the Norse Hel, for that matter). Orcus could also mean the land of the dead; from Orcus' association with death and the underworld.

Time - Dimensional Travel:

42487 Angstrom: Angstrom Levy was a comic book character with the ability to travel to alternate realties after a horrible accident with technology.

Note: *this asteroid is traditionally used to depict "angst", unease, or anxiety in charts.*

8330 Fitzroy: Trevor Fitzroy was a comic book character with the ability to absorb another person's life force, and create space or time portals.

274020 Skywalker: fictional character from "Star Wars" movie series. Could take the name literally as "Sky Walker". One who walks with the stars in the sky. Astral projection. Space travel.

3325 TARDIS: Time and Relative Dimension in Space (time machine).

15332 CERN: Associated with time travel, portals, frequencies, dark/anti matter. Ripples in time. Turning back time. Changing or altering timelines.

Fun personal note: *in my chart- Skywalker, TARDIS, and CERN are all conjunct with a 1-degree orb. All three trine my natal Neptune and South Node at Galactic center. I've always joked, I'm just here trying to find my monolith/portal back home.*

12448 Mr. Tompkins: is a character in a series of four popular science books by the physicist George Gamow. The books are structured as a series of dreams in which Mr. Tompkins enters alternative worlds where the physical constants have radically different values from those they have in the real world. The aim was to use these alterations to explain modern scientific theories.

The Adventures of Mr. Tompkins:

1.) He began his day at a lecture about the theory of relativity. The lecture bores him, and he drifts off to sleep in a dream world in which the speed of light is slowed down and he is traveling faster than those objects around him. (Time travel/altered timelines.)

2.) He spends time as a conduction electron, returning to consciousness when he is annihilated in an encounter with a positron. (In simple terms it's an explanation of the particle collider at CERN that is used to produce anti matter aka dark matter.)

Note: there is such a thing as 4D time matter; time crystal or space-time crystal is a structure that repeats in time, as well as in space. Normal three-dimensional crystals have a repeating pattern in space but remain unchanged as time passes. Time crystals repeat themselves in time as well, leading the crystal to change from moment to moment.

Keywords: altered state of consciousness; remote viewing; time travel; crossed timelines; multi-dimensional ascension; quantum physics; dream downloads; the Matrix. Frozen in time. Mad scientist. Quantum physics research. Escapism. Dissociation. Losing track of time. Erratic behavior.

If this asteroid is in strong aspect to Neptune, Uranus, or Jupiter, the more influential way this asteroid affects the personality.

35734 Dilithium: A substance of great power in the science fiction universe of Star Trek. Dilithium is an essential component for the faster-than-light warp drive depicted in the stories. In the original series, dilithium crystals were rare and could not be replicated. In the real world, dilithium is a molecule consisting of two covalently bonded lithium atoms.

It's possible this could represent time travel, astral projection, duality representing a parallel universe (Di meaning two) example: CERN and the "god particle".

5405 Neverland: there are many rumors about what the real "Neverland" is. Some say it's a map of the child's brain. It was to represent immortality, escapism and never growing up. Think about the present-day virtual reality video games. Or a simulated reality. Technology has become Neverland. It's now a major part of our brains and it downloads/updates us daily. Technology remains immortal, not humans (yet).

3276 Porta Coeli: "Heaven's Door," or gateway to heaven. Portal to the next life or a portal we used to get here consciously.

446 Aeternitas: Roman goddess. The divine personification of eternity. "Limitless time." She is associated with virtue (morally good). She is sometimes represented by the phoenix, symbol of cyclical time, since the phoenix was reborn in flames every 500 years. Immortality. In numerology, the number eight represents infinity, merging the material and spiritual worlds together. Crossing timelines. Resurrection; regeneration.

Side Note: Some have used this asteroid in synastry charts to reveal the possible length of the relationship. (I have not personally verified this.)

69230 Hermès: in this instance we are using Loki the trickster with the tesseract. He walks between worlds teleporting himself and sometimes others. Loki possesses extrasensory abilities and is capable of astral projection and casting his thoughts across great distances; and across dimensional barriers, even if he is unable to move. Additionally, he is known for his ability to shape shift.

85585 Mjolnir: Thor's hammer, is used as a teleportation device allowing him to access wormholes in time and pass-through portals. It can control the weather, uses energy sensing, protective barriers, and energy absorption with redirection.

1922 Zulu: The Zulu tribe in Africa claim that space travelers called the "Nommo" gave them advanced knowledge. The Zulus say the Nommo are air-breathing, amphibious beings, like frogmen; complete with scales.

The Ancient Sumerians also recorded accounts of these Nommo aliens coming from space on their 6,000+ years old stone tablets and cylinder scrolls. The Zulus claim that the Nommos taught them advanced knowledge of our solar system and the Sirius star system which is 8.6 light years away.

Specifically, a dark star named Sirius B, which is only visible from Earth with advanced technology.

The Zulus and the Dogon knew of this dense dark star and its exact orbits hundreds of years before modern astronomy. They also have complete knowledge of the size, colors, and several moons of the planets in our solar system.

They claim this knowledge was given to them by the Nommos from Sirius B. The constellation falls in between 5°-18° Cancer, however 14° Cancer is the exact location for Sirius.

Ideally, use these asteroids to locate connections and what is it communicating with in your chart to send, receive/download messages etc. How does it "teleport" you through life? When we were born, we were in a sense "teleported" here.

Technology is advancing faster than light. It's reached quantum levels, and these breadcrumbs are nothing compared to what has already and is already happening. This is all because "time" itself is being altered by a continuous quantum universe.

We already do live in a parallel reality. We don't need to move parallel, we may need to go nonparallel sort of like "anti-matter".

Asteroids in Astrology Simplified

1246 Chaka: **(Shaka)**: king of the Zulus who was ahead of his time regarding innovation and social reforms. Shaka changed the nature of warfare in Southern Africa from a ritualized exchange of taunts with minimal loss of life into a true method of wholesale and complete slaughter. Some saw him as a hero, others saw a monster.

Norse/Celt:

(Finnish, Germanic, Pagan, Gaulish, Slavic, and Celtic)

16912 Rhiannon: Celtic Moon goddess. Queen of fairies. She is the goddess of fertility, rebirth, wisdom, magic, transformation, beauty, artistic inspiration and poetry. Fantasy romance.

3989 Odin: is the god of wisdom, poetry, war, death, divination, and magic. Known as the All Father.

456 Abnoba: Gaulish goddess of childbirth as well as the patroness of all waterways. She is the protector of woods, springs, rivers, and wild animals. She's known as the goddess of the Black Forest. Is sometimes identified as Diana (Roman) Huntress.

Note: *If harshly aspected by a malefic transitioning planet, the shadow side could manifest as losing a child during childbirth or miscarriages.*

385 Ilmatar: Finnish goddess, born of the air, created the universe from seven cosmic eggs. She was a virgin goddess, but following her impregnation by the wind, gave birth to the gods of music, magic, and smithing. Creation and literal fertility (fertile eggs) are associated with her. Her connection with the wind ties her to floating or resting; possibly flying.

178 Belisana: Celtic goddess, identified with Minerva. Her name translates to "brightest, strong one".

Keywords: bravery, strength, ancient wisdom; bright light.

11284 Belenus: Gaulish god of light, with responsibilities to sheep and cattle. Celtic Sun god. Called the "fair shining one". He was one of the most ancient and widely worshipped Celtic deities. Also associated with the ancient fire festival and modern Sabbat Beltane. He was said to ride the Sun across the sky in a horse-drawn chariot; (Greek equivalent to Helios). Belenus is considered a god of healing, wisdom, light, and prophesy. Celtic version of Apollo.

8034 Akka: Finnish earth mother and goddess of harvest and feminine sexuality. Fertility.

Keywords: renewal, highly sexualized feminine energy; nurturing mother; receive nourishment.

471143 Dziewanna: (Devana) is the Slavic goddess of wild nature, forests, and the hunt. She is the equivalent to the Roman goddess Diana. Associated with spring and agriculture. There is much debate among scholars (aka egos) on the meaning of her name and existence. The consensus is that her name translates to "virgin, maiden, god and wonder. Giver of Life". She is wild and free, mistress of horses, who rides through the land awakening the plants and banishing the winter crone. Her hair is always wild and never bound. This is noteworthy, because she is married, and at the time in Slavic history, married women wore their hair tightly bound. She is the iconic woman, like Lady Godiva who broke the chains for women in her culture. She may have been married, but there was equality in her marriage. A confident, self- reliant, stable warrior woman who returned every spring, from the land of the dead to tend to the crops. She's going to be your "don't give a shit or take any shit" placement in the chart. Divine healing.

Additional Note: Dziewanna is also tied to a very important healing plant, called the Mullein. Used in medical astrology.

621 Werdani: Norse Norn of the Present (current day). Here and now.

1130 Skuld: The "future", named after one of the three Norns (fates) in Norse mythology. Represents futuristic outlook, psychic foretelling/seer of future. Determines the inevitable future fate of mortals, North Node energies, water-spirit. past-present-future, divination, our fate, our life's direction, our future, the outcome, what is to come, prophetic.

167 Urda: Norn of the Past; possible past life recall; esp. through dreams if south Node/Neptune/Moon are strongly aspected.

894 Erda: connected to "fate", some scholars believe she is a combo of all the Norse Norns as Urda posted above . One story says that Urda is the oldest goddess of the three Norns, a trio of sister goddesses associated with the past, present, and future. They were believed to help mothers as they gave birth and ruled over a person's unchangeable destiny. Solution to the questions posed; other movements mirrored other outcomes.

2462 Nehalennia: goddess of the ocean. She is related to trade, the sea, ships, and the harvest of the sea itself. She rules over passage from one state to another, such as the transitions from living to death.

126 Veleda: a priestess and prophet of the Germanic tribe of the Bructeri. Sorceress with powers to immortality in the magical world away from reality. Name possibly translates to "prophetess".

Keywords: prophecy; seer; sorcery and magic; divination; veil between worlds; psychic; *knowing*.

131 Vala: as female shaman and seer in Norse religion.

77 Frigga: goddess renowned for her ability of foreknowledge, or what we would call precognition or psychic abilities. With a name meaning "beloved", Frigga is associated with love and desire. She is also known as a goddess of wisdom and is associated with the element of earth.

It is known that she was a volva, or seeress and sorceress, and that she brought the Norse magic of Seidr to the gods and mankind. Seidr is the art of altering the woven course of one's destiny, which was achieved by entering a state of higher consciousness, very similar to that of Shamanism. Seidr was primary a feminine activity, and practitioners would travel from village to village performing seidr in return for food and shelter.

76 Freia: like Frigga in some interpretations. Also known as "The Lady", was the Norse goddess of love, war, and beauty. She had a twin brother Freyr, and together they were the chief gods of the Vanir. She was a master of Seidr (magic) and is the wife of Óð. Freyja was the leader of the Valkyries, who would ride over battlefields to choose slain warriors to rest in Freyja's Hall (the rest going to Odin's hall Valhalla).

240 Vanadis: additional name of the Norse goddess Freyja; same as Asteroid 76 Freia. A goddess associated with love, sex, beauty, fertility, gold, war, and death.

242 Kriemhild: Norse princess (also called Gudrun). Kills her husband to avenge her brother's death.

Keywords: vengeful; holding grudges; unforgivable actions; protective of siblings.

657 Gunlod: in Norse mythology, she was the daughter of a giant. She was in charge of guarding the gate of poetry or art. *In astrology, she is said to be where hidden talents are to be discovered or "unlocked".*

135 Hertha: Norse goddess; sometimes called Nerthus; fertility; hearth; and home. Earth goddess/goddess of cows. Overall goddess of household management; hospitality; and a helpful peacemaker.

Often associated with Yule and Christmas time. Hertha's themes are rebirth, kinship, health, longevity, and tradition. Her symbols are dormant trees and snow. Home comfort and security. Nourishing.

601 Nerthus: Norse goddess of fertility. (See Hertha above)

699 Hela: goddess of the dead and what is "hidden". Underworld.

949 Hel: Norse goddess of the dead; same as "Hela" above.

256 Walpurga: infamous German witch; also known as "The Lady of May Day". Walpurgis night and how a woman went from Catholic saint to Germanic goddess, to witch and gave us a second Halloween. Represents changing/evolving spiritual beliefs; mystic; healer.

122 Gerda: Norse goddess associated with the Earth. Like the Persephone myth with ties to the underworld and famine.

Keywords: being bounced back and forth between people or scenarios; stuck in the middle; used as a bargaining chip; used in power plays; jealousy from other females; no control over your own life.

1260 Walhalla: Hall of the Chosen Dead. (Norse = Valhalla.) The "privileged or rewarded souls" place of rest.

4895 Embla: First female human in Norse mythology. Her male counterpart is Ask. The gods bestowed upon them various corporeal and spiritual gifts. Represents creation of humans formed from trees. Embla (elm tree) or "vine". Norse "water pot". Mother of mankind. *"The Insight of the Seeress."*

4894 Ask: Male counterpart of Embla Some use them as a pair in synastry. Creation. His name is derived from "ash tree".

2155 Wodan: Norse god of war; Ancient Germanic sky god. Wodan was known as Woden or Wotan to the Saxons, and later Odin to the Norse. He was not only the god of war; he was the god of victory in battle.

Associated with war, thunder, battle.

4059 Balder: Norse god Baldr. He is the son of Odin and Frigga (who foresaw her son's death). He is the god of light, joy, purity, and the summer sun, also considered "daytime". He was so handsome, generous, and good that he gave off light simply by the purity of his character.

Keywords: charm, charisma, kindness, high intelligence and wisdom. Fearless. Brave. Pure heart or pure love. Exquisite beauty. Light workers. Precognition or prophetic dreaming. Fair and just.

4669 Hoder: blind god, twin of Baldr. His brother Baldr was loved and well respected. Some versions say Hoder was used as a pawn to kill his brother, others say he went into the underworld to get a special weapon worthy of killing his brother.

Keywords: sibling rivalry. Jealousy. The "shadow" side of one's personality. If looking at the story allegorically, they could be viewed as the same person (Jekyll and Hyde).

Note: *I would look at these two asteroids as a pair, to see where one shines and where one buries secret desires or fantasies. Asteroid Balder is 4059.*

4092 Tyr: Norse god of war and the lawgiver of the gods. The bravest of the gods, and the god of justice. His day is Tuesday. He is most like Mars. Tyr showed himself to be the foremost god of law by sacrificing one of his arms to uphold it.

Keywords: war, law and justice. Honorable military leader.

4179 Toutatis: Celtic god, or "tribal protector". Often depicted as extremely blood thirsty. The alters are depicted as very bloody human sacrifices. With extremely violent acts of torture rituals to appease the god. Barbaric acts.

Keywords: this asteroid could show strongly in a violent crime chart where a victim was slowly tortured to death. It may show in a chart of a cult leader who demanded human blood sacrifices. Ritual murders, etc., someone who is literally blood thirsty.

14960 Yule: traditionally associated with Christmas, but "Yuletide" or Yulefest" is of pagan roots signifying winter solstice and winter festival; connected the celebration to the Wild Hunt, the god Odin (Norse).

Usually means "winter feast".

877 Walkure: in Norse mythology, a Valkyrie is one in a group of female figures who decide which soldiers die in battle and which live. Warrior, fearless and strong female. Athletes. Disciplined.

15810 Arawn: The Celtic god of the dead, war, revenge and terror within the Welsh mythology. He reigns supreme as the ruler of the spiritual realm of Annwn.

4213 Njord: Norse god of sea, merchants, wind, and fertility and wealth; husband of Nerthus (Mother Earth). Some event astrologers link this asteroid to severe flooding storms. He was usually invoked before setting out to sea on hunting and fishing expeditions. He is also known to have the ability to calm the waters as well as fire.

H55 Vulcan: Norse god of fire, volcanoes, metalworking.

(Hypothetical Point.) Refer to Uranian astrologer for additional interpretations.

4862 Loke: cunning trickster and mischievous. Associated with the planet Mercury. Intellectual, communications, technology, transportation. Asteroid Loke, with natal Mercury or Uranus can present a genius, high IQ, eccentric out of the box thinking. These minds are made for plotting, strategy and can sell the devil holy water.

176 Iduna: goddess of eternal youth, reigns over the orchards. Represents health and rejuvenation. Agriculture and healthy food.

Note: shadow side could present as eating disorders or self-depreciation behaviors when in harsh aspect to other planets and chart points.

4484 Sif: Earth goddess (wife of Thor). Scholars have proposed that Sif's hair may represent fields of golden wheat; she may be associated with fertility, family, wedlock, she is connected to rowan, the sacred tree.

Asteroids in Astrology Simplified

343 Ostara: goddess of spring and fertility, renewal, rebirth. (Easter).

4572 Brage: god of writing and poetic arts, music, and creativity.

3990 Heimdall: watchman or messenger of the gods. Called the "shining" god. Required little sleep. Always alert.

4599 Rowan: Norse "tree of life". Interesting symbolism for sure, as the tree is "roots" and "origins", sort of like DNA. Rowan is one of the most sacred trees used by the Celts even today. It's noteworthy that Rowan is used in the famous Beltane festival, we know as "May Day". They believed the tree had many healing and magical qualities.

85585 Mjolnir: Thor's hammer/weapon. Power, communication and transportation.

2176 Donar: Thor, god of thunder.

428694 Saule: Baltic solar goddess whose story is said to be equivalent to Rapunzel. Light deity damsel trapped away in need of rescue.

9325 Stonehenge: sacred Druid ritual site. I like to notate the transit location of this asteroid during important equinox/eclipse phases. For example, it was conjunct the Sun in a solstice chart that I pulled.

3037 Alku: Finnish for "beginning".

1705 Tapio: forest spirit or god in Finnish mythology. Hunters prayed to him before the hunt. God of nature. He was a shamanic god who could teach a lot about the mysteries of nature and the healing powers of herbs and trees. He also spoke the language of all forest animals, for they were all part of his kingdom.

Keywords: nature-loving, outdoor lifestyle. Hunting. Cabin in the woods, getaway. Spiritual connection with trees, forests, and flora. Herbal healer. Listening to nature.

394 Arduina: Arduenna, Gaulish goddess of the Ardennes forest and region. Thought to be represented as a huntress riding a boar. Similar to the Roman goddess Diana.

Keywords: freedom, independence, strength, strong connection with nature, nurturing, stability, growth.

140 Siwa: Slavic goddess of life and fertility. Her name means "living, being, existing". Fruitful.

5164 Mullo: Celtic god associated with Mars; "Mars-Mullo". He had a cult following with several shrines. Mullo is also associated with horses, it is Latin for "mule". Partial symbolism referring to one of the four horsemen in Christianity. One was a red horse, the god of war (Mars). He is most notably acknowledged for his ability to heal the eyes (eyesight). Symbolically, the opening of one's third eye, as his shrines depicted the eye symbol.

Keywords: spiritual warfare; finding enlightenment after significant battle; taking action; finding inner strength.

Mullo plot twist: Mullo is a vampire in Roma folklore. It translates to mean "one who is dead" or "undead". A Mullo is created when a person dies suddenly of some unnatural cause, or the person did not have proper funeral rites. A Mullo is described as having white clothes, hair that reaches their feet, and one physical oddity (varies on geographic region). A Mullo's existence is in seeking out people it did not like in life and harassing that person. Mullos are believed to return and do malicious things, and attack by strangling and sucking the life blood of a person (usually a relative), who caused their death or disrespected them after death.

Shadow Side: hauntings; revenge; Gothic culture; disrespecting the dead; karma; bloody violence.

5370 Taranis: Celtic god to whom human sacrifices were made. Many representations of a bearded god with a thunderbolt in one hand and wheel in the other have been recovered from Gaul, where this deity came to be syncretized with Jupiter. Mostly recognized as the god of thunder, like Thor.

1460 Haltia: (Haltija) is a spirit, gnome, or elf-like creature in Finnish mythology that guards, helps, or protects something or somebody. They are sometimes called fairies and are separated into many "spirit" categories based on their magical powers. Healing using the elements (air, fire, earth and water). There is also one specifically for the dead.

4250 Perun: Slavic god of thunder and lightning. His other attributes were fire, mountains, wind, rain and storms. The oak tree, iris flower, and divine messenger; the eagle (spirit). He is strongly attributed to making weapons with stone and metal. Norse equivalent to Thor. In later mythology, a cult of Perun developed believing in human sacrifice to Perun would bring them the most powerful weapon on earth.

481984 Cernnunos: the conventional name given in Celtic studies to depictions of the "horned god" of Celtic polytheism. Cernunnos was a Celtic god of fertility, life, animals, wealth, and the underworld. They believed he reflects the seasons of the year in an annual cycle of life, death, and rebirth. Some say he took time to comfort the dead by singing to them on their way to the spirit world. He is sometimes misunderstood or misrepresented as Satan by modern religion because of his horns. This is far from the truth and worth noting.

Asteroids in Astrology Simplified

Keywords: protection, strength, grounded, transformation, cycles, wisdom, hunting, fertility, comfort, nurturing, gentle giant; sacred wisdom. Similar traits of the earth signs: Taurus, Capricorn, and Virgo.

Be gentle and kind, relying on your own wisdoms and truth. You are braver and more protected than you may think.

52963 Vercingetorix: was a king of the Arverni and military leader of the Celtic people against the Roman invasion. He raised an army of the poor and made alliances with other tribes. He beat Julius Caesar's forces at the Battle of Gergovia but surrendered during the battle of Alesia, presumably because of superstitions related to the lunar eclipse or to save as many of his men as possible he gave himself to the Romans. Name translates as "great warrior king".

Keywords: very superstitious. Self-sacrificing. Leader. Respected. Loyal. He was fighting against the elite on behalf of the poor village people who stood no chance on their own. He was resourceful. Kind. Took care of the underdog. Protective. Taking a stand against injustices and unfairness.

116 Sirona: is a Celtic healing goddess associated with snakes and eggs, and healing springs of water. Just like those healing springs, her story runs so much deeper. She had a massive underground cult following. She was usually depicted as holding her large snake as it feeds from eggs in a bowl from her hands. Sirona's image is parallel to that of the Greek goddess Hygeia. (Giving health.) The snakes feeding on eggs are symbolic of regeneration and rebirth. It could also be a symbol of fertility.

Sirona: "She who makes us better."

The star goddess kept watch over a healing spring of water. She kept it flowing with life, full of fish for the village to feast on, she provided the right amount of light for the vegetation to grow which provided the healing herbs needed for medicine.

Sirona in the natal chart could represent a place you seek healing, sacred wisdom, and transformation. It's not a wound like Chiron. It's where you go to be healed. It's your sanctuary. Your healing spring. Where you "level up". Rejuvenate. Regenerate and recharge your own batteries.

2091 Sampo: The Sampo is a legendary device in Finnish mythology. One interpretation is that it was a magical astrolabe; the most common interpretation is that it is the World Pillar or World Tree. The World Pillar is a mythical column on which the precession of the spring equinox turns. "Sampo highlighted in the natal chart also gives an understanding to astrological principles, and ability to see connection in the heavenly movement of planets to themes of our lives. Sampo gives us an understanding of the mechanics of the heavenly movements and the skills of the astrologer in respects to drawing up and preparing charts." — Source: Neptune's Astrology Website.

471926 Jormungandr: world snake in the depths of the ocean, a giant serpent/dragon. Jormungandr is biding his time. Prophecies tell us that he will merge at the end of time to destroy the nine worlds of Norse mythology, but for now he is merely waiting.

He is the offspring of Loki, and was tossed into the ocean by Odin.

He encircles the entire globe, reminiscent of the ancient symbol we all may be familiar with the snake/serpent in a circle looking as if it's eating itself. This was called Ouroboros in ancient depictions and is associated with the underworld. The prophecy says that when he releases his tail, Ragnarok (the final battle that results in the destruction and subsequent rebirth of the world) will begin. Thor the god of thunder is his arch enemy.

One sign for the coming of Ragnarok is the violent unrest of the sea as Jörmungandr releases its tail from its mouth and thrashes its way onto land. One half of the world will be on fire while Jörmungandr sprays poison to fill the skies and seas of the other half. Here is where the last meeting between the serpent and Thor is predicted to occur. Thor will become occupied with battling the serpent and is unable to help others as they fight their own battles. He will eventually kill Jörmungandr but will fall dead after walking *nine* paces, having been poisoned by the serpent's deadly venom.

The world snake Jormungandr is trying to wake the world up. Shake us from our deception. Break us free from our chains.

__Ouroboros__ is the symbol for infinity, a cycle of rebirth and regeneration. I once noted, when I wrote about Jormungandr that he represents cycles of "time" and transits with him are very important. These cycles are where you may find something that you repeat over again.

A personal theory is that Jormungandr is the metaphorical equivalent to the earth's equator going all the way around earth. The great "equalizer" and if/when he decides to rise that would be "Ragnarok". What is interesting to note between the Norse and Hopi prophecies is that they both mention the number "nine" as the final signs. Nine is symbolic in bringing the Earth's three worlds together in a state of finality before it begins all over again. Jormungandr is trying to wake the world up. Shake us from our deception. Break us free from our chains.

Additional Notes:
- Jormungandr, the "world serpent" is in the most spiritual and original cosmic bodies of water (fixed star Nunki). Furthermore, it is a "hot blue star", symbolic of a "blue Kashina" from the Hopi prophecy.
- The Hopi Tribe calls the seventh planet the Red Kachina, and it's moon the Blue Kachina.
- The Sumerians called it the Great Red Dragon. Hebrew was the Destroyer.
- The Winged Serpent by Ancient Indians and by the Egyptians the Winged Disk.
- Other names: Winged Orb, the Death Star, Planet X.
- It was considered by the Babylonians to be the celestial body associated with the god Marduk.
- Extraterrestrial race referred to in the Bible as fallen angels and called the Anunnaki, "those who from heaven came to earth" in Sumerian.
- Aka "The Nephilim". They were the offspring of the "sons of God" and the "daughters of men" according to Genesis.
- There are many parallels with the Hopi prophecy and Norse prophecy. The great serpent "destroyer" they both describe could very easily be Jörmungandr, the "Nephilim" son of the Norse god Loki.
- Additionally, fixed star Nunki associated with the Anunnaki. This fixed star is located at 12 Capricorn, in the Sagittarius constellation. Notably, this fixed star is an ambitious blue dwarf star- in it to win it.

Keywords: cycles. Where something may repeat over again. Beginnings and endings; transformative; humanitarian efforts; unity; becoming one. Are you breaking the cycle or stuck in one?

Shadow Side: judgmental; not listening to others or giving fair chances. No patience; lack of humility; bully; misunderstood.

Recommended to look at transits in charts of significant events.

Prophetic Gift:

126 Veleda: a priestess and prophet of the Germanic tribe of the Bructeri. Sorceress with powers to immortality in the magical world away from reality. Name possibly translates to "prophetess".
Keywords: prophecy; seer; sorcery and magic; divination; veil between worlds; psychic; instinctual knowing.
131 Vala: a female shaman and seer in Norse religion.
12312 Vate: Italian for prophet or fortune teller; divinely inspired writer.
29314 Eurydamas: an elder of Troy, had the gift of prophesying dreams, but could not foretell the death of his sons.
65583 Theoklymenos: Greek seer; people laughed at his predictions not knowing they would in fact be killed that night.
Keywords: prophesy, visions, enlightenment, foresight; not believed; knowing something will happen, can't change fate.
10247 Amphiaraos: was a seer and greatly honored in his time. Both Zeus and Apollo favored him, and Zeus gave him his oracular talent. His name translates to "doubly cursed". He would show strongly for someone with psychic or prophetic ability.
13 Egeria: goddess of prophecy; our ability to access the wisdom of our ancient forefathers. It shows how we can spiritually reconnect to past belief systems as symbols, puzzles, and archetypes that help us to understand who we are.
16974 Iphthime: was Penelope's sister who appears to her in a dream and comforts her as she is grieving. Messages delivered via dreams; communicating with loved ones who are deceased; encouragement and reassurance from the spirit world.
9106 Yatagarasu: the holy crow, or raven with three legs of Japanese mythology. The crow/raven represents divine guidance and prophecy.
4227 Kaali: prophetic dreams and can open the door for a psychic attack if the energy is not used properly. The gift here would be a very risky one to take on and most likely a highly evolved soul, because of the violence and shadow world connections.
22533 Krishnan: (Krishna) most popular of the Hindu gods. Is revered as a supreme deity and the eighth incarnation of the god Vishnu. Worshiped as a restorer of order to the world; prophecy foretelling of what is to come; also, something that is predicted.

108 Hecuba: prophecy that came with a cost of grief and loss.

5264 Telephus: telepathy; communication; how one receives and gives messages.

14827 Hypnos: prophetic dreams; visions/memory recovery/healing using hypnosis. Dissociative states of consciousness.

4197 Morpheus: god of dreams; prophetic dreaming, and interpretation.

114 Kassandra: the seer whose voice goes unheard. Kassandra's curse, that no one would believe what she saw/said while trying to warn others about situations. Where someone tries to warn others but isn't believed.

432 Pythia: Oracle of Delphi; divination prophecy.

408 Fama: Oracle of Delphi and dream prophecy; communicator between realms.

1862 Apollo: god of prophecy and healing; cursed Kassandra.

4679 Sybil: Greek, priestess with prophetic powers; the wise one.

168 Sybilla: Greek priestesses with prophetic powers; Divine Guidance.

148780 Altjira: prophetic dreams; shamanic.

Note: presence is strongly felt when transitioning natal Neptune, Moon, or Jupiter.

7 Iris: rainbow messenger goddess of the sky and sea. Iris has a twin named Arke (no asteroid.) It's important to know that Arke is Iris's twin by being the "other side of the bridge", and to know/use Iris you still must understand Arke. Iris is the astral traveler to the heavens or underworld and Arke is her tether to find her way back to earth.

77 Frigga: goddess of wisdom and foreknowledge.

106 Dione: a mother goddess who presided over the oracle at Dodona.

3240 Laocoon: was a famous seer in Greek mythology, it is assumed that it was Apollo who gave Laocoon the skills needed to see into the future. But he was murdered when his vision/advice was misinterpreted by the gods.

4138 Kalchas: the most famous soothsayer among the Greeks at the time of the Trojan War. It had been predicted that he would die when he met his superior in divination; the prophecy was fulfilled.

1130 Skuld: Norse Norns (prophets) of fate; seers of future.

167 Urda: Norn of the Past; possible past life recall; esp. through dreams if south Node/Neptune/Moon are strongly aspected.

894 Erda: same as above (Urda).

4341 Poseidon: heightened prophetic gift sensitivity; channeling especially connected to Neptune.

8405 Asbolos: a seer, prophet who read the signs of nature for his people. This could indicate a person's ability to tap into "the spirit of the times"; those who have futuristic knowledge of events or trends and can anticipate the outcome. **Note**: their advice or input is sometimes rejected as being ahead of its time. Strong intuition; psychic gifts. *(See additional information under the "Bird List" asteroids for Asbolos.)*

8060 Anius: son and priest to Apollo. Apollo cared for Anius for a time, teaching him the arts of divination and prophecy. Anius later became his priest. He had three daughters who could turn into wine, seed, and oil.

Keywords: prophecy, wisdom. Occult. Wise sage. Family provider. Trusted advice. Alchemist.

73769 Delphi: location of the famous Greek Oracles of Delphi; sacred grounds; ritual work.

382 Dodona: the other oracle location for the high priestess of Zeus and other gods. Sacred/ritual grounds.

569 Misa: Greek divinity in the Orphic Mysteries. A mystic female version of the god Lakkhos. There seems to be a consensus that she could relate to gender identity. As a deity of the Orphic Mysteries, Misa is sometimes understood as both male and female.

Keywords: oracle, prophecy, obscure, secretive, hidden identity, mysterious.

4660 Nereus: the father of the Nereids. (Old Man in the Sea.) He is described as a shapeshifter with the power of prophecy. Powerful mystic.

215 Oenone: mountain nymph; name translates to "wine woman". Her gift of prophecy and healing was learned from Rhea. Her lover, Paris, abandoned her for Aphrodite. When he returned home wounded from war, begging for her to heal him with her gifts, she refused, and turned him away to die. Later, she felt remorse and committed suicide.

Keywords: prophecy; seer; healing arts; stubborn; loyalty.

Shadow Side: selfish; not using gifts to help treat everyone equally; holding grudges; finding out revenge is not worth the moral weight; could be used to indicate suicide. Regrets.

Additional note: sometimes she is used along with asteroid Paris #3317 to indicate tumultuous relationships; infidelity; unforgiveness.

Note: *The word "psychic" is used very loosely and easily these days, just like the word "empath". So, my hope here is that we dig deeper in helping each other truly understand their own unique gift of intuition and insight. There are many layers of what being "psychic" truly is.*

LGBTQ:

I've done a lot of thinking about this list, and wanted to get it right. As we all know many of these asteroids are interchangeable, and just because they land on one "list" does not deem them to be just one thing. If you consider the broadness of the LGBTQ community and the movement itself, I simply ask that this list be used with an open mind. At times, the list may become highly sexualized. The reason for that is because of the sexual transformation and sexual revolution that naturally crosses over into this movement.

The Muses in mythology: Sappho was the one most written about and has been given the most attention when looking at synastry or LGBTQ qualities in a person's chart. However, I'd like to point out, that ALL the Muses were used for something, and they should be considered in my humble opinion, as they all represent some form of art. Art can be sexual or intimate etc., depending on how you personalize interpretations and impressions.

1863 Antinous: also called the "gay god". Known for his beauty. He was the lover of Hadrian, the first openly gay emperor. There is a new age underground movement following that has formed again with worship to Antinous.

80 Sappho: symbol of female homosexuality (lesbian). From the island of Lesbos, known for lyric poetry. Wild and free spirited. Hypersexual.

1036 Ganymede: usually used as a model for homosexual behavior between an older adult male and younger male. It can also just represent homosexuality. Or being attracted to older/younger same-sex partners.

11965 Catullus: 1st century Roman poet; the explicit sexual imagery which he uses in some of his poems has shocked many readers. The erotic poems are about his homosexual desires and acts, but most are about women. Some of his poems were very crude, vulgar, and obscene. He greatly admired Sappho and was the source of what we know about her.

Keywords: writer, poet; homosexuality; bisexual; erotica; crude; pornography; sexual desires. If harshly aspected, possibly a hard time expressing one's fetishes in a healthy manor or feeling shame for having certain desires.

125 Liberatrix: to liberate. Freedom. To release. The freedom to be who you are without restriction. This could depict BDSM, sexual fantasies.

569 Misa: Greek divinity in the Orphic Mysteries. A mystic; the feminine version of the god Lakkhos. There seems to be a consensus that she could relate to gender. As a deity of the Orphic Mysteries, Misa is sometimes understood as both male and female. "She is the goddess with characteristics of two genders, that she is a queen, and a powerful one at that. She has been depicted as having the quality of purity. Considering her possible conflation with Cybele, it seems she is a Great Mother type of deity." ~ *Internet Source*

Keywords: obscure, secretive, wholesome; caring; nurturing; gender related, possibly she could be a transgender goddess.

98 Ianthe: whose name translates to "purple or violet flower". Her lover, Iphis, was a female, but raised as a male. Iphis was in love with Ianthe and begged the gods to allow the two females to be married. Her wish was granted, when Hera changed Iphis into a man, which allowed them to be married. *This would have technically been a possible first example of sex change.* Asteroid could show up strong in charts where one undergoes a sex change operation.

12258 OscarWilde: a popular Irish poet and playwright in the 1800s who had a notorious gay lover named Lord Douglas (Bosie). The relationship was wild and reckless, flamboyant, full of gambling, drinking, break ups, and reconciling. Astrologers have used this asteroid to pinpoint homosexual tendencies in charts.

149 Medusa: this would show up in a chart for sex change or dramatic change in physical appearance. An extreme transformation has taken place. Maybe if one just likes to cross dress. Change appearance.

3671 Dionysus: Greek god of ecstasy. Excess pleasure. There is much evidence in the Dionysian Mysteries to know what took place behind closed doors. I hate to be cliche, but this is probably where "in the closet" originated. And I do say that with the utmost respect. They threw out societal standards and lived behind closed doors to experience and express a sense of freedom without limitations and restraints. Each person experiences this asteroid differently in their own chart. In this case, it could be where one experiments sexually without limits. Bisexual. Open relationships.

433 Eros: god of love and desire.

Eros was depicted as an adult male who embodies sexual power, and a profound artist. Sometimes called the "Renaissance Cupid". Since the beginning of record history, myths, folklore, and all sacred texts have incorporated themes of same-sex eroticism and gender identity; myths often include homosexuality, bisexuality, or transgenderism as a symbol for sacred or mythic experiences. Unbridled passion.

1809 Prometheus: god of forethought. Tricked the gods (Zeus) by switching out creation genitalia in a game to beat Zeus and win. This is another well-known story of transgenderism and/or sex change. This asteroid would most probably be the catalyst for that change. Or the forethought (thinking about) getting the change done.

588 Achilles: was in a homosexual relationship with Patroclus and favored him the most. Although it's not so out in the open, this is a place where you may find tender loving relationships taking place behind closed doors and not out in the public eye. It could also be a place where one cheats on one's heterosexual spouse and finds meaningful healing and identity their soul seeks.

4450 Pan: The god is still worshipped in some underground LGBTQ circles today. Pan frequently was depicted in sculpture chasing both women and men around with his always-erect penis and oversized scrotum. Half man; half goat. Bisexual.

12606 Apuleius: a writer/philosopher and was an initiate in several cults or mysteries. The most famous incident in his life was when he was accused of using magic to gain the attention (and fortune) of a wealthy widow. Most of his writings are about experiments with magic. He was very active in The Dionysian Mysteries, a ritual of Ancient Greece and Rome which sometimes used intoxicants and other trance-inducing techniques (like dance and music) to remove inhibitions and social constraints, liberating the individual to return to a natural state.

Keywords: occult; divination; magician; fortune teller in an "unethical" way; trickster; free spirit; adventurous; liberator; willing to try anything once; life of the party; where one loses inhibitions or where one is used for the sake of the experiment; reminds me of the Fool tarot card.

12607 Alcaeus: was a Greek poet. He was an older contemporary and an alleged lover of Sappho, with whom he may have exchanged poems. Alcaeus' reference to Sappho in terms more typical of a divinity, as holy/pure, honey-smiling Sappho.

Alcaeus was like a mentor to Sappho. A deep-rooted friendship that used each other as muses for their own poetry and expressionism.

Keywords: mentor; friendship; comedy; poetry and writing (maybe romantic comedy). Reminds me of a Venus in Gemini who may prefer relationships of intellect over the physical act itself; someone who prefers watching sexual exploits but does not actively participate. Voyeurism. Asexual. Abstinence. Intellectual sexual curiosity.

2102 Tantalus: thirst for temptation and desire. This could be a dark place of abstinence tendencies that may be unhealthy depending on how the chart is aspected. (Many other things must be taken into consideration here.) Self-mutilation for abstinence. Experimentation with sexual preference.

Apollo, Hermès, and Hercules are also widely known to be playboys. But tracking down and explaining their conquests would be longer than writing the Iliad itself.

To keep things simple:

Apollo 1862: certain aspects could show bisexual energy. Appreciation of sexual freedom. Engaging in many sexual encounters.

Hermès 69230: certain aspects could show the double life (half as the faithful heterosexual spouse and half as the homosexual fling). Don't forget he's tricky to pin down. Always on the move. Experimenting. Needing to taste the rainbow... (literally).

Hercules 5143: had many male companions in his long journey. Bisexual. Homosexuality.

Lilith:

Note: Lilith's in placement and aspect can depict sexual desires and preferences, but it takes experience to read and interpret the Lilith correctly. For that reason, I just place them here with short summaries.

1181 Lilith: asteroid Lilith. Temptation; internal conflict; subconscious shadow; dark fantasies. Interpreted like BLM Lilith.

Notes on Lilith:

Lilith in a man's chart does represent the woman he secretly desires, but fears. Femme fatale/dominatrix comes to mind, the association with BDSM. In a woman's chart, it's said that Lilith represents unbridled passion, a certain wildness and inhibition, fiercely independent and sexual, along the lines of a sexuality that is unconsciously projected.

Waldemath Lilith: also called "Dark Moon Lilith"; not an asteroid. This is an energy/hypothetical point proposed in modern astrology. Sometimes described to be amorphous, with vague feelings and/or a sense of dread. Desire for retribution or revenge; leaning too heavily on old/outdated habits; dwelling on the past; vague and mysterious. It has very Neptunian qualities when being activated by transits. Often described as a "dust cloud" only visible at certain times. Are you running from a real problem or one that may not really exist?

Love, Lust, and Sex:

Quote from an online article:
"In my view, the natural progression of Love is from Eros to Philia, to Agape. One has undeniable and obvious affinities for certain people, places, and things. This is Eros. By engaging our natural Eros while also seeking "right relationship" with the objects of our affections, we avoid the possessive shadow manifestations because we are truly concerned about the well-being of the other as much or more than ourselves. It is only when we have mastered the right relationship of Philia that we can approach Agape without unconsciously or unintentionally engaging the dangers of the transpersonal realms." -*Source: Mountain Astrologer (Faces of Love.)*

433 Eros: passion, desire, lust, Divine Masculine version of love. Sexual desire; lust; often used in synastry with asteroid 16 Psyche (soul mate). The sign and house Eros is in may represent what a person truly wants and desires in a mate or what they most certainly do NOT want. Aspects to Psyche, Venus, Mars and Nodes are important to note. If Eros is square Neptune, this person may have unrealistic standards/expectations in partners.

280 Philia: means "brotherly love" or friendship; affection. Aristotle believed to feel the highest form of philia for another, one must feel it for oneself; the object of philia is, after all, "another oneself". The term is widely used in the "egoism" movement, what is a healthy dose of ego?
Keywords: love, fond friendships, not the erotic kind of love. Strong soul bond. True self love. The place you do self-discovery and lose the not self-ego. Pure of heart.

5023 Agapenor: means: "unconditional love", "soul love"; heart chakra; not sexually or lust driven; pure essence of love.

268 Adorea: adoration; to adore; admire.

21029 Adorno: means "ornament" or decoration. Garnish. Fancy. Elaborate. Excess. Bold. Flamboyant. Ostentatious. Embellish; extra.

44821 Amadora: means "gift of love" in Italian; or a lover, sweetheart or suitor in Spanish.

390 Alma: Means "soul". Could indicate a "soul bond" when aspected to Venus, Mars, or the Nodes. Additionally, if Alma is conjunct the vertex/anti vertex it could represent past life soul bonds.

4847 Amenhotep: Egyptian pharaoh, god of architecture, buildings, and construction, translates to "Amun is satisfied".

Keywords: linked to love/relationships in synastry charts, past life connections, other possible associations: rebuilding, architecture, foundations, mortuary, funeral rituals, revolutionary visions, trendsetters and followers. ***Note***: *religious persons say "Amen" after prayers.*

8267 Kiss: kissing; displays of affection and attraction.

966 Muschi: German term for "kitty", or sexual slang for "vagina". It could also be used as a term of endearment or nickname for one's partner.

1585 Union: to come together; partnership; marriage; friendship; joined resources.

51663 Lovelock: union; love connection. The lovelock was a long lock of hair, often braided and made to rest over the left shoulder (the heart side) to show devotion to a loved one.

61342 Lovejoy: love and joy; happy and content.

161215 Loveday: a day of love; interesting if this is strong in wedding day charts. For example, if it is conjunct Venus or Mars. Conjunction or aspecting a planet in the 7th house, on the day of marriage.

33685 YoungLove: young love; new relationship; developing love interest.

447 Valentine: love with martyr undertones; one partner may sacrifice more for the other; avoidance of confrontation through compassion.

4 Vesta: the sacred flame, love, all things sexual, fertility, passion, desire, purity, Divine Spark, fire, devotion, loyalty, focused, sacrificial, dedicated. Putting personal needs aside, self-sacrifice, service, integrity, and truth. High priestess, spirituality.

1236 Thais: a famous Greek "companion" or "prostitute" who accompanied Alexander. She's famous for instigating the burning of the palace at Persepolis She is said to have been very witty and entertaining. An educated harlot living outside the system.

Keywords: free spirit, clever, creative, musical, artist, entertainer, sexual companion (friends with benefits). Independent. Well-traveled. Life of the party. Non-conformist. Instigator. Initiator. Muse of inspiration.

868 Lova: lovers; love; possibly superficial intimacy; quick hook ups.

73511 Lovas: lovers; love; possibly superficial intimacy; quick hook ups.

432971 Loving: care deeply about; comfort; compassion; kind love.

90703 Indulgentia: Latin for "indulgence, goodness, kindness, love, tenderness, fondness". Also the gratification of another's desires, inclinations or humors. Where we indulge ourselves.

728 Leonisis: Leo N Isis (Leo and Isis) ~ fun find! They combined Leo with the goddess Isis. Isis embodies spiritual kundalini, unity, love, loyalty, and resurrection while Leo rules royalty, kings/queens, ego and passion. Isis would be almost exalted in Leo. Isis personified as the rising phoenix! Pure unrestrained raw power.

11965 Catullus: 1st century Roman poet; the explicit sexual imagery which he uses in some of his poems has shocked many readers. The erotic poems are about his homosexual desires and acts, but most are about women. Some of his poems were very crude, vulgar and obscene. He greatly admired Sappho and was the source of what we know about her.

Keywords: writer, poet; homosexuality; bisexual; erotica; bold and expressive sexual actions; pornography; shocking sexual desires.

Shadow Side: possible sexual abuse or addition; angered when can't' sexual perform; extremely perverse fantasies. If harshly aspected, possibly a hard time expressing one's fetishes in a healthy manner or feeling shame for having certain desires.

202 Chryseis:
Keywords: being held captive against ones will; staying in a bad relationship too long; being used as a bargaining chip or leverage in a situation out of one's control. Learning when it's best to let one go, or suffer consequences of holding onto something for selfish reasons. Knowing when to let go. Biding time. Ransom. The consequence of selfishness and ego. "Crisis."

240 Vanadis: additional name of the Norse goddess Freyja; same as Asteroid 76 Freia. A goddess associated with love, sex, beauty, fertility, gold, wealth.

1036 Ganymede: goddess of homosexual love; passion; desire; lust.

211 Adonis: god of beauty and desire. Used a lot in synastry charts.

128 Nemesis: fate, cosmic debt enforcer; equalizer; used in synastry.

7328 Casanova: seductive; flirtation; temporary hook up; selfish or superficial pleasure.

499 Venusia: Venus; devotion; beauty; love; romance/relationship. Depending on the house and aspect to the planet Venus, could indicate a hidden Venusian quality not seen on the surface at first glance.

16 Psyche: used in synastry charts alongside Eros and Cupid for love lost and found again; reunited. Karmic relationship cycles; breaking free or remaining in a karmic loop depending on aspects of Venus, Neptune, and the Nodes.

Note: *Psyche's interpretation is interchangeable, not just for use in synastry. See other possibilities under "Most Popular Asteroids" list.*

206 Hersilia: figure in the foundation myth of Rome. She is credited with ending the war between Rome and the Sabines. She was deified, as Hora Quirini. She wept at the loss of her husband in battle, and Juno made her a goddess to be united with her husband in the sky.

Keywords: peace maker, loyal, wanting the best possible outcome; where one is willing to make compromises on behalf of family; strength and harmony. Negotiator; devotion; self-sacrifice.

398 Admete: "Unbroken", "unwedded", or "untamed".

Note: *some connect this asteroid with Admetus.*

H40 Cupido (hypothetical point) and 763 Cupido (asteroid): love at first sight; instant attraction; romantically involved; manifested love; sparks fly, undeniable magnetic attraction; fun and playful; "new love".

62 Erato: muse of romantic poetry.

24994 Prettyman: literally a pretty man; physically attractive.

367 Amicitia: enamored; friendly; kind; amicable; magnetic.

1221 Amor: amor is not unconditional, neither is Venus. They are about love and depending on placements and aspects, both are easy to fall in and out. More an objectifying love.

8490 Companion: partner; friendship or romantic; trusted friend.

4580 Child: may indicate having children in natal charts; or one's inner child. With certain aspects, it can depict how one experienced childhood.

562 Salome: daughter of Herodias, who famously requested the head of John the Baptist after Salome danced for Herod. Her dancing brought him so much pleasure, he granted her mother anything she desired.

Keywords: femme fatale; empowered female; "Lilith in broad daylight", enchantress; mistress; provocative dance; alluring siren; sex appeal; lust and desire. Fantasy woman; wears many costumes; performer in exchange for favors. Natural people pleaser. Used by own mother to provide. (Look for aspects to the Moon.)

174 Phaedra: represents lust for another person's partner; emotional infidelity; unable to handle rejection; vengeful; covetous; using sex as a manipulation tactic; temptations.

19631 Greensleeves: An old English folk song. One possible interpretation of the lyrics is that Lady Green Sleeves was a promiscuous young woman and perhaps a prostitute. At the time, the word "green" had sexual connotations, most notably in the phrase "a green gown", a reference to the grass stains on a woman's dress from engaging in sexual intercourse outdoors.

An alternative explanation is that Lady Green Sleeves was through her costume, incorrectly assumed to be sexually promiscuous. Her "discourteous" rejection of the singer's advances supports the contention that she is not.

Keywords: promiscuity; "lady of the night"; sex work; judgements based on appearance; being a target of sexual harassment; sending the wrong message. Green is associated with fertility. Green is also traditionally associated with money, finances, banking, ambition, greed, jealousy, and Wall Street. It could also represent social status.

65 Cybele: The universal mother of not only the gods but also of all humans, animals and plant life. Her story is complex and has an aura of mystery surrounding her. Traditionally, "mother" would be interpreted as nourishing and kind. If Ceres is the traditional mother standard, Cybele is the anti-tradition mother figure. She was wild, untamable, and "uncivilized". Similar qualities to Lilith. Her rituals were lively with instruments, frenzied rhythmic dancing and screaming.

Keywords: healing using shadow work, spiritual rituals; free spirit, non-conformist. Sexual freedom. Sexual spiritualism: using sex to transcend spiritual and physical boundaries set by society. Secret/mysterious work. Mysticism and spell work.

169 Zelia: feminine form of Zelos, Greek god. He and his siblings were winged enforcers who stood in attendance at Zeus' throne and formed part of his retinue.

Keywords: personifies dedication, emulation, eager, rivalry, envy, jealousy. The English word "zeal" is derived from this name. Intense devotion. Guardian. Too much enthusiasm. Extreme passion. Obsessive.

8009 Beguin: means "to have a crush on someone".

Keywords: crush. Admirer. Infatuation. Enchanted. Flirtation. Enamored. Fond. Obsess over. Fantasize about.

767 Bondia: Roman goddess Bona Dea, chastity and fertility, healing, and protection of Rome. She was worshiped solely by women, and her cult allowed for women to do things they were otherwise not allowed to in Roman society, such as drinking.

Keywords: The tie that "binds" or whatever is "bonded" to this area in one's chart. Divine feminine power; non-conformist. It has been used to represent bondage willingly such as BDSM. Or some form of restraint for sexual preferences.

Shadow side: to be bound unwillingly; kidnapped; tied down.

236 Honoria: daughter of a Roman emperor; gained a reputation of being ambitious and promiscuous, using her sexuality to advance her interests. She seduced her chamberlain, but their affair was discovered, and she was sent to a convent. She plays many games to avoid being married off.

Keywords: free-spirit; ambitious; stubborn; rebellious; manipulative; cunning; seductive; using sex to get one's way; selfish; playful; power plays; gambling; risk taker; troublemaker; black sheep of the family; rejecting societal standards. Her name literally means "honor", dignity, grace, integrity. Possibly a ruined reputation for not doing as told; victim of gossip and lies. In modern times, this could be a person accused of using sex for personal advancements. Mistress or homewrecker.

545 Messalina: Roman empress, wife of Claudius. The empress without principle. Pornography. Promiscuity.

To call a woman "a Messalina" indicates a devious and sexually voracious personality. The historical figure and her fate were often used in the arts to make a moral point, but there was often a prurient fascination with her sexually liberated behavior. One story tells of her all-night sex competition with a prostitute, to which the competition lasted for twenty-four hours, and Messalina won with a score of twenty-five partners. Another story says the empress used to work clandestinely all night in a brothel under the name of the She-Wolf.

Additionally, This asteroid may indicate a political scandal or be used for smear campaigns to discredit another person's reputation with accusations that may not be true. As noted by historians, "accusations of sexual excess were a tried and tested smear tactic and the result of politically motivated hostility."

Keywords: sex worker; sexual addictions; insatiable; infidelity. Unable to control sexual impulses. Victim of exaggerated rumors to hurt someone's reputation; liberation; unusual sexual proclivities; lowered inhibitions; sexual fantasies.

493 Griseldis: from European folklore, Griselda noted for her patience and obedience. Her story is very tragic. When she marries, her husband tested her obedience by demanding she give up her children. She obeys without protest. Then her husband no longer wants her, and he divorced her, and sent her back to live with her father. (She went obediently.) Some years later, her husband announces he will remarry and calls her back to be the servant. He introduces her to a twelve-year-old girl he claims is to be his bride, but who is really their daughter. Griselda wishes them well. Finally, he reveals their grown children to her and Griselda is restored to her place as wife and mother.

Keywords: patience, and obedience in the most extreme sense. Enduring much suffering, remaining loyal and faithful to personal and societal morals. Eternal faith everything would work out. Humble. No self-confidence. Doormat. No inner authority. Being able to endure hardships as a test of faith. Possible Stockholm Syndrome towards abusers.

3 Juno: "the loyal wife" traits; devotion and fidelity. Many use her in synastry charts.

103 Hera: the Roman version of Juno (above). Usually portrayed as the ideal wife in a marriage. She was devoted, even when betrayed. Most will say she was vengeful but always faithful. What is intriguing is the fact that Hera's "super strength" was feared by Zeus himself. Her healing powers were also unmatched. Her shadow side could be considered cold, vengeful, vindictive, and ruthless.

72012 Terute: the faithful and wise wife. She was a princess who was sent to work in a brothel after her husband died. She took on the house chores, and any menial duty to keep from having to have sex with other men because she was still in love with her deceased husband. He eventually comes back from the dead, grotesquely disfigured and unrecognizable. He discovers how she has remained faithful and humble. They eventually end up together happily ever after.

Keywords: faithful relationship; loyalty; widowhood; keeping the faith; accepting physical deformities; overcoming the odds. There is a certain strength and resolve in her story. Her morals and ethics remained solid even in the hard times. An unwavering hope and faith that it will all be ok.

673 Astarte: a version of Venus or Ishtar. Queen of Heaven. Goddess of love, fertility and war. Her symbols are the lion, horse, and chariot. The consensus is that she is more symbolic of war, rather than "love". However, love is historically known to be one of the most passionate reasons for war. As the saying goes: "in love and war".

3497 Innanen: meaning "Lady of Heaven", "Queen of Heaven and Earth." Represents both the morning star and evening star (Venus). Symbolic of her decent and ascension to heaven from the underworld, where she had to pass through the seven gates of hell. She can be viewed as a powerful warrior fighting towards the Light and the Divine feminine within.

1388 Aphrodite: associated with Venus. The goddess of love, lust, beauty, pleasure, passion, and desire. She is also the patron goddess of prostitutes/sex workers which led scholars to propose the concept of "sacred prostitution". Animal associations include the dolphin, sparrow, blood of a sacred dove, swan, hare, goose and butterfly. Symbols include roses, seashells, a pearl mirror and myrrh.

211 Isolda: love, infidelity, lust, affairs; love at first sight; "honeymoon phase".

1387 Kama: god of love; desires; Kama Sutra; spiritually sexual encounters.

328 Budrosa: rosebuds typically symbolize beauty, youth, innocence, purity. The bud symbolizes something getting ready to bloom or blossom. Not yet ripe. There are also references to a rosebud representing the female clitoris. In literary history, it's been used as a pet name for "mistress". The word rosebud was that of losing one's sexual innocence, or being a "prized possession". This isn't always a negative, it can be beautiful to watch planted seeds bloom. Parents watch their children, girls, becoming a woman, or boys becoming a man all the time. *Interpretations would vary depending on the aspects or the "environment" where Budrosa is found in one's chart.*

1291 Phryne: accused of impiety, lack of proper respect for something considered sacred. It was believed that impious actions such as disrespect towards sacred objects or priests could bring down the wrath of the gods. *When it seemed as if the verdict would be unfavorable, her attorney removed Phryne's robe and bared her breasts before the judges to arouse their pity. Her beauty instilled the judges with a superstitious fear, who could not bring themselves to condemn "a prophetess and priestess of Aphrodite" to death. They decided to acquit her out of pity.*

Keywords: acquittal; wrongly accused; to be made an example of; exquisite, divine beauty. Getting your way based on looks; judged because of being pretty, petty power plays.

192 Nausicaa: mythological Greek princess from the Odyssey. Her name translates to mean "burner of ships". Theme of unrequited love or "love never expressed". Her father tells Odysseus he would let him marry her but no romantic relationship takes place between the pair. Nausicaä is also a mother figure for Odysseus. She ensures Odysseus' return home, and thus says "Never forget me, for I gave you life.", indicating her status as a "new mother" in Odysseus' rebirth. She is also attributed to the invention of ball games.

Friedrich Nietzsche, in Beyond Good and Evil, said: "One should part from life as Odysseus parted from Nausicaa—blessing it rather than in love with it."

Keywords: deep connection, non-romantic relationship. To treasure a friendship so much, you don't want to ruin it by expressing feelings. Modern day "friend-zone". Playfulness, protection of friends; requited love.

5129 Groom: married groom.

19029 Briede: the bride and groom (married.)

Mysticism & Magic:

34 Circe: mystic, magic, sorcery, enchantress, herbal healer, alchemy, assisting others with witchcraft. Wisdom and sage advice. Covens. Secret gifts passed down through ancestral roots. Divination and spells. She had the ability to rearrange matter itself, and trained Medea in the healing arts in the temple of Hecate, honoring the goddess of the dark night and magic.

212 Medea: known as the "wise one" for her skill of healing and proficiency using drugs and herbs. She was trained by Circe in the arts of sorcery, magic, and herbalism; expert in spell casting to rearrange matter. She was also a priestess in the temple of Hecate, honoring the goddess of dark night and magic. Medea was an expert on the Moon and timing the lunar cycles to draw power from the moon for rituals and ceremonies.

Keywords: feminine wisdom that intuitively knows how to cooperate with nature and its cycles. She instinctually knows the right time to perform rituals to evoke the healing spirits or exorcize demons. When prominent in the natal chart, she can reveal the need to explore ancient feminine traditions using witchcraft, herbalism, and spell casting. She would be especially powerful with a strong aspect to the Moon or Venus. Medea reminds us to honor ancient customs and respect nature.

100 Hecate: triple Moon goddess; supreme sorceress.

432 Pythia: priestess at Delphi; using snakes or poison to summon messages; divination practices.

407 Arachne: spiders are used in some healing arts; also considered seers. Being good at a particular craft; shape shifting; magic of writing, those who weave magic with the written word. (Divine messages received through the web.) Arachne carries several meanings, one instance is having a natural born talent or gift that is extreme and draws attention. It must not be boasted or bragged about. It can draw in jealously and envy from others. Natural mystic. Dreamcatchers.

Note: In modern times, she could be the metaphorical "world wide web" aka Internet. Used for good and bad. Falling into a web of danger.

277 Elvira: "Mistress of the Dark"; vampire fantasy.

7464 Vipera: seems to be connected to witchcraft/vampire themes. It is worth pointing out the obvious: this can show up in snake bites and poison. In research, I have found that people who have asteroid Vipera conjunct natal Mercury tend to weaponize words, metaphorically "spit venom" when upset or angered. This also includes, when transit Vipera conjuncts an individual's natal Mars, Mercury, or Pluto.

8964 Corax (raven): ravens are considered auspicious messengers; wise prophetic powers; teacher or partner in magical studies.

337380 Lenormand: French fortune teller known for tarot cards.

148780 Altjira: dream god connected to mysticism and shamanic abilities.

4257 Ubasti (Bast): Egyptian cat goddess; goddess of protection, fire, passion, birth, dance, music, and the home. Some pagans call upon her when in danger and need of protection or passion.

42 Isis: goddess of motherhood, magic and protector of the dead.

577 Rhea: magical healing or prophetic powers.

10199 Chariklo: prophetic, compassion, protection magic, mystic bloodlines; magic healing; shamanic. (Chiron's wife). Look for a connection to Chiron and Vesta. She worked closely with Vesta and Athena to amplify protection and strength. Chiron (Divine masculine) healing, while Chariklo (Divine feminine,) to balance (Ying/Yang) healing practices.

3897 Louhi: is described as a powerful and evil witch queen ruling over the northern realm of Pohjola, with the ability to change shape and weave mighty enchantments.

Keywords: enchantress; divination, occult, spell work, alchemy; sorcery; witchcraft/magic; quests; healer, Divine healing techniques; mystery.

3606 Pohjola: the mythical realm that queen/witch Louhi ruled.

699 Hela: goddess of the dead and what is "hidden". Underworld.

949 Hel: Norse goddess of the dead; same as "Hela" above.

256 Walpurga: infamous German witch; also known as "The Lady of May Day". Walpurgis night, and how a woman goes from Catholic saint to Germanic goddess, to a witch and gave us a second Halloween. Spiritual enlightenment.

375 Ursula: an underwater version of Medusa; the sea witch from the Disney movie, The Little Mermaid; selfish and insecure tendencies. Vindictive and manipulative.

149 Medusa: inflict terror or fear; overcoming trauma; protecting those who are weaker; seeing all sides to the story; turning weakness into unbeatable power; misunderstood; if she is prominent near Venus, Moon, or Lilith, the person may constantly face jealous or insecure females. If Medusa is in close aspect to natal Mars, Saturn, or Pluto, the person may experience intense power struggles with men/authority figures. She can be a shield or a weapon. Additionally, if she squares Neptune or Poseidon (the reason for her curse), could indicate a person here to heal and live the life of a survivor.

2696 Magion: magic; magician; spell work, manifesting.

136818 Selqet: the goddess of fertility, nature, animals, medicine, magic, and healing venomous stings and bites in Egyptian mythology; originally the deification of the scorpion. Her name is translated to mean "she who tightens the throat or restricts breath" but it could also mean "she who controls breath and causes the throat to breathe".

Keywords: using herbal medicines to induce trance like states for visions. Bridging the psychic and alchemy realms together; projection and protection. Healing using poison. Death by poison.

18032 Geiss: (geas): a geas is compared with a curse, or paradoxically, a gift. If someone under a geas violates the associated taboo, the wrong doer will suffer dishonor, or even death. On the other hand, observing one's geas is believed to bring power. Often it is women who place geas' upon men. In some cases, the woman turns out to be a goddess or other sorceress figure.

Keywords: curse, spell, hex, magic, mystical or supernatural, controlling power; inherited gifts; prophetic fulfillment, restriction, manipulation, superstitious; inducing fear.

2091 Sampo: the Sampo is a legendary device in Finnish mythology. One interpretation is that it was a magical astrolabe. The most common interpretation is that it is The World Pillar, or World Tree. The World Pillar is a mythical column on which the precession of the spring equinox turns. "Sampo highlighted in the natal chart also gives an understanding of astrological principles and ability to see connection in the heavenly movement of planets to themes of our lives. Sampo gives us an understanding of the mechanics of the heavenly movements and the skills of the astrologer in respects to drawing up and preparing charts."

— Source: *Neptune's Astrology Website*

1049 Gotho: goth or gothic. The medieval "vampire" culture. The Goths were east Germanic peoples who mainly played a role in the fall of the Roman Empire. Well-known for their detailed architecture with intrinsic and artistic craftmanship. Often associated with paganism.

Keywords: dark; revival; underground organizations; medieval style and couture; color black; vampirism; uncivilized or against popular society norms. Finding beauty in the darkness. Lover of night.

579 Sidonia: a noblewoman who was tried and executed for witchcraft. Legends depict her as a "femme fatale". Known as "Sidonia the Sorceress". She and her friend remained unwed and travelled around like gypsies supposedly casting spells, fortune telling, and having "satanic" sexual encounters. What made her famous was the mysterious ways her entire family died off leaving no generation to carry the bloodline forward.

Keywords: non-conformist; free spirit; captivating and charismatic; adventure seeker; world traveler; restless; wanderlust; enchantress; curses and spell casting; divination; superstition; "man eater", possibly willing to commit crime and murder.

12606 Apuleius: a writer/philosopher who was an initiate in several cults and mysteries. The most famous incident in his life was when he was accused of using magic to gain the attention (and fortunes) of wealthy widows. Most of his writings are about experiments with magic. He was very active in The Dionysian Mysteries; a ritual of ancient Greece which used intoxicants and other trance-inducing techniques combined with music and dance to remove inhibitions and social constraints; liberating the individual to return to its true natural state.

Keywords: occult; divination; magician; unethical "fortune telling"; trickster; free spirit; open minded; adventurous; liberation; willing to try anything once; where one loses inhibitions or where one is used for the sake of "experiments". Losing consciousness and possible addiction indicator. Not knowing one's limits.

12619 Anubelshunu: Anu Belshunu was a lamentation priest and interpreter of the astrological omen series Enuma Anu Enlil at the Temple of Anu in Uruk. A collection of astrological cuneiform tablets from his library contains some of the earliest realistic depictions of Babylonian constellations. His work deals with Babylonian astrology that interprets a wide variety of celestial and atmospheric phenomena in terms relevant to the king and state.

Keywords: astrologer; astronomer; historian; predictive prophetic instincts; futuristic messenger; wise council and advisors to those in high political places; someone who interprets for a living.

873 Mechthild: Mechthild of Magdeburg, medieval German mystic, "The flowing light of the godhead." The first mystic to write in German. Composed seven books total of her visions with the Divine light god. She lived with the community of Cistercian nuns at Helfta, who were considered highly educated and gifted mystics. She was later recognized as a saint who is the patron against blindness. Additionally, she was known to be musically gifted with a beautiful singing voice, and was sometimes called "The Nightingale".

Keywords: mystic; writer and translator; one who leads people to the light (enlighten). Prophecy, person who listens, sees, and shares knowledge and wisdom with natural enthusiasm and charisma.

3315 Chant: rhythmic phrase. Spellbind. Repeat. Reciting tones. Lyrical speech. Ritual practices for mantras, prayers, or spells.

514 Armida: from an Italian poem by by Torquato Tasso. She was a pagan sorceress. Armida was sent to stop the Christians from completing their mission and is about to murder the sleeping soldier, but instead she falls in love. She creates an enchanted garden where she holds him as a lovesick prisoner. He eventually is rescued from her spell by his fellow Christian soldiers. In some versions, Armida is converted to Christianity, in others, she rages and destroys her own enchanted garden. She represents the "abandoned woman" and is sometimes compared to Circe the enchantress.

Keywords: sorcery, magic, casting forbidden love spells. Using one's powers to control someone else for your own satisfaction. Manipulation, witchcraft; seduction, and self-destruction. Keeping someone against their wishes. Spiritual warfare. Enchanted gardens.

30 Urania: goddess of astrology.

18032 Geiss: curse or spell prohibiting an action.

12312 Vate: fortune teller; palm reader.

4227 Kaali: Kundalini awakenings.

2598 Merlin: wizardry; divination; witchcraft; spells; ancient wisdom of the arts. Sacred traditions. (See Fairy Tale list for in depth details.)

174567 Varda: character/angelic goddess of the Divine light; ascended light worker.

131 Vala: female shaman, or seer in Norse mythology.

25115 Drago: dragon; from the Draco constellation; auspicious powers.

24168 Hexlein: means "little witch" in German; to hex or spell cast.

Fairy Tale and Fictional Character:

Fairy tales often serve as mirrors to our deepest hopes, fears, and desires. The themes that run through them reflect timeless aspects of human experience itself.

545521 Aladdin: original story from "One Thousand and One Arabian Nights". Possibly receiving help from unexpected or divine sources; going on a journey of spiritual awakening; being blessed and giving back. Coming up from nothing and creating greatness for yourself and others. "A whole new world."
Shadow side: being easily tricked to take a short cut, or greed.

28494 Jasmine: is technically named for the flowering jasmine plant. She is also from the Disney movie "Aladdin" and the story of "One Thousand and One Arabian Nights". Her personality is to follow one's heart and not accept old traditions of arranged marriage. Symbolic of breaking free of an archaic social belief, being in control of one's own destiny/path. Her beliefs and intelligence is more futuristic and clashes with current outlooks. Female embodiment of empowering and inspiring others to conquer fears, restraints, and outdated systems. Bold not passive. Take charge. She chooses excitement and adventure over comfort and stability. Very similar to Venus in Gemini archetypes.

1224 Fantasia: Disney film. The final sequence depicts the triumph of light over darkness, goodness over evil.

824 Anastasia: Greek name meaning "resurrection". Overcoming an obstacle. A recurring theme of Anastasia is the importance of finding and being true to yourself. For Anastasia, the play is a journey toward self-knowledge.

15845 Bambi: an Italian term from "bambino" meaning "baby." Being prey to a predator. Animal rights advocates. Victimization. A hard childhood, with struggles for survival. Bambi overcoming harsh environments and obstacles, particularly physical limitations. Loneliness. *The deer spirit animal symbolizes a connection to the inner child; it also teaches kindness and love.*

9500 Camelot: mystical castle of King Arthur.
Keywords: code of morality and good faith. An idyllic place filled with joy, happiness, and peace. Where those seek refuge from reality.

Escapism.

2598 Merlin: magician from the legend of King Arthur. Wizardry; divination; witchcraft; spells; ancient wisdom of the arts. His most notable abilities commonly include prophecy and shapeshifting. Sometimes depicted as a wild, or "mad man". He embodies a conflict between knowledge and power. Master alchemist. Sacred geometry and energy healing.

On the negative side: Merlin could appear that being honest with people is beneath him and that commoners don't deserve to know the truth. Manipulation through magic or illusion. Feeling morally superior and thus exempt from laws of honest conduct. (Look for his shadow side asteroid #57658 Nilrem)- which is Merlin spelled backwards. Mirrored The Merlin was sacred to the Welsh god of prophecy, Bran the Blessed, whose head was oracular. Also to Freya who wore a cloak of falcon feathers. The Merlin carried messages from the dead. The living patterns of our genetic heritage, preserved as memory to our current state of consciousness. He is oftentimes seen as the wild card; as the breaker of enchantments who ironically got trapped within his own enchantments when he fell in love and got locked up in a tree for his efforts. He is here to remind us how important it is to maintain spiritual and physical balance, while achieving self-mastery and enlightenment.

57658 Nilrem: Merlin spelled backwards. As in evoking spells in reverse. Wizardry. Illusions. Mirrored projection. Shadow side of Merlin.

2497 Arthur: King Arthur is said to have led the Knights of the Round Table at Camelot in the 5th or 6th century. He has come to represent moral integrity, loyalty, and defending the weak.

2041 Lancelot: knight of the Round Table in King Arthur legends. Known as the "proud one." Lancelot was known for his loyalty and chivalry, and was the lover of Queen Guinevere. Courtly love and temptations. Lancelot's adulterous love for Guinevere causes him to fail in his quest for the Holy Grail, and sets in motion events that lead to the destruction of the Round Table.

14238 D'Artagnan: character in The Three Musketeers novel by Alexandre Dumas. Master of the sword. Defender of the weak. Military prowess. Strategic thinker. Strong protective instincts.

Keywords: leadership; loyalty; confidant, and protector who earns respect and trust. Skilled tradesman. Wise. Proving oneself worthy. Starting from the bottom, working way to the top. Persistent; "never give up" attitude. Honorable.

9499 Excalibur: legendary sword from the King Arthur tale. Symbolism of acquiring "superpowers" when using them for the highest good. A tool for positive transformation that must be metaphorically "unlocked" deep within us after putting in the work. Like finding the key to unlock Chiron.

Note: *look for aspects to Saturn, Pluto and Chiron.*

4017 Disneya: named after Walt Disney himself; visionary.

256369 Vilain: every story has a villain. This could be where we are victimized or beat our own demons. Survival. Receiving harsh criticism or having someone sabotage our efforts.

Note: *follow the transit to see if it is in harsh aspect to Pluto (power struggle), Mars (abuse), or Venus in a relationship.*

1773 Rumpelstiltskin: folk tale character. The imp who bargained with a girl held captive by a king. He saved her life by spinning straw into gold with the condition she gives up her first born to him. When he came to collect the child, she couldn't part with her newborn, and so the imp told her if she can guess his name, she can keep her child. When he realizes he has been beaten at his own game he becomes enraged and flees. The name Rumpelstilzchen in German means literally "little rattle stilt." A stilt being a post or pole that provides support for a structure. A rumpelstilt or rumpelstilz was consequently the name of a type of goblin, also called a pophart.

Keywords: spirit or poltergeist, mischievous spirit that clatters and moves household objects. Trickster. Up to no good. Greed. Riddles and games. Lessons learned; don't be greedy, don't lie, and don't make promises you can't keep.

3514 Hooke: Captain Hook is the villain to Peter Pan's hero in the novel Peter and Wendy. Metaphorically, it is theorized that Captain Hook represents death, while the crocodile represents time, and both are the forces that Peter Pan avoids because he never ages (immorality.) He could represent defeat or surrender. Possibly a thought cycle of someone who is "hooked" or fixated on someone/something.

695 Belle: main character from Disney's movie Beauty and the Beast. Belle's name means beauty, and she is portrayed as a woman who is beautiful, both inside and out. The song "Belle" has a theme of how society treats those it deems differently.

Keywords: pure, inner goodness. Empathy. Independent. Brave and unafraid of social stigmas.

Shadow side: judging a book by its cover. Not giving people chances. Prejudices.

12410 Donald Duck: Disney character; known for having a temper or an exaggerated emotional response to problems. He teaches us to overcome adversity through perseverance.

Keywords: quick to anger; impatient; insecure; moody; pessimistic outlook; not giving up.

4487 Pocahontas: in the Disney movie she is the daughter of Chief Powhatan. She fears being possibly wed to Kocoum, a warrior whom she sees as too serious for her own free-spirited personality. After having a dream about a spinning arrow, Pocahontas visits Grandmother Willow, a talking willow tree that alerts her to the arriving English. She became the symbol of peace between her traditional roots and the "new world".

Keywords: connected to nature; spirit guides; messenger between worlds; peacekeeper; adventurous and open- minded. Bridging a gap.

18932 RobinHood: legendary English archer and outlaw of Sherwood Forest who with his band of Merry Men, robbed rich unscrupulous officials to aid and protect the poor in what might be described as a medieval form of socialism.

Keywords: maybe prominent in politicians or activist charts. Humanitarian. Standing up for the little guy. Fighting for a cause. Against oppression and greedy regimes. Social injustices. Living "off grid." A person who devotes themselves to volunteer work. Compassionate.

17627 Humpty Dumpty: reminds us that great power brings enemies and risk to those who climb too high without having checks and balances. No one is invisible. Sometimes you must take the fall and accept a new path.

12927 Pinocchio: the obvious connection to lies, perhaps a part of life we find superficial. Where we can be naive or where we want to feel "normal"; also possibly a physical abnormality that "sticks out".

94 Aurora: damsel in distress, a part of our subconscious that is in a metaphorical sleep. Sleeping Beauty. Hidden enemies. Susceptible to poisoning.

375 Ursula: manipulation of the innocent, lies, stolen voice. (Villan in the Disney movie The Little Mermaid.) Underwater version of Medusa.

Keywords: jealousy, envy, vanity, insecure, and hidden enemy; vindictive.

16626 Thumper: where we might be optimistic or confident. Always in a rush, excess nervous energy- makes me wonder if this would be prominent in a chart for someone who literally nervous taps their foot or has any quirky nervous ticks. Indicative of anxiety and hyperactivity.

428694 Saule: Baltic solar goddess whose story is said to be equivalent to Rapunzel. Light deity, damsel trapped and needing rescue. Finding the light at the end of the tunnel. Perseverance, never losing hope.

12623 Tawaddud: fictional character from medieval Arabian stories or One Thousand and One Arabian Nights. She was a talented slave-girl from Baghdad whose knowledge of astronomy, medicine, theology, and alchemy. She was superior to that of the best scholars in the court. Smart, witty, brave, beautiful, fearless, daring, assertive, and proactive. A woman of substance and depth in a world that suppressed instead of celebrated success and evolutionary knowledge. Breaking the glass ceiling.

12608 Aesop: Aesop's Fables; stories that contained wisdom and indoctrination. Earliest form of propaganda for religious, social, and political themes.

5405 Neverland: There are many stories about what the "real" Neverland represents. Some say it is a metaphorical map of a child's brain. It was possibly meant to represent immortality, escapism, and never growing up. Our inner child. Where do we find happiness? Fantasy- driven idealism. Not living in the real world. Augmented reality.

775 Lumierre: The candelabra light character in Disney's movie Beauty and the Beast. Represents optimism, light, shine. Illumination.

543 Charlotte: one of the main characters in the book Charlotte's Web by E. B. White. The name means "free man" or "petite." In the story, Charlotte is a spider who befriends a farm pig named Wilber. She writes messages on her web praising Wilber, in hopes the farmer lets him live. She died of exhaustion right after saving his life. She was praised as a hero and looked upon as "Divine intervention".

Keywords: looking out for the underdog, angel in disguise, small blessings, messages received in mysterious ways, guardian angel. Modern days, networking through the world wide web.

15109 Wilber: the farm piglet; runt of the litter who is in danger of being slaughtered in Charlotte's Web. Name means "willful, bright."

Keywords: the outcast, bullied, given a second chance, escaping death. Underdog that doesn't give up or dwell on what can't be changed.

16421 RoadRunner: bird that darts in front of fast-moving cars; reckless; impulsive; rushed behavior; always in a hurry; on the run from something. Mischief.

182 Elsa: snow queen in the Disney movie Frozen. Elsa has the magical ability to create and manipulate ice and snow. She inadvertently sends Arendelle into an eternal winter on the evening of her coronation. Throughout the Frozen film, she struggles first with controlling and concealing her abilities, and then with liberating herself from her fears of unintentionally harming others, especially her younger sister. *Note*: Asteroid Elsa may be named after the character in the legend of Lohengrin. In the story Loherangrin arrives in a boat pulled by a swan and offers to defend her, though he warns her she must never ask his name. He weds the duchess and serves Brabant for years, but one day Elsa asks the forbidden question. He explains his origin and steps back onto his swan boat, never to return.

225088 SnowWhite: is technically a "dwarf" planet. The third largest dwarf planet in our solar system with its own moon.

Snow White is Freyja. Freyja and her "seven dwarfs" are symbolic of the seven days of the week which construct the lunar week.

In the 1937 Disney movie Snow White, the symbols surrounding the magic mirror were the twelve zodiac signs. Snow White was the representation of purity and goodness prevailing against vanity and evil.

Keywords: choosing to take the higher ground or the longer route to achieve lasting results. Fighting against superficial human desires. Overcoming adversity against all odds while maintaining integrity. The dwarfs represent a strong support system that can be found outside the traditional blood related family. Love conquers all. Metaphorical reflection of humanity.

Note: medically, it could show up in an actual poisoning case.

Operation Snow White was a criminal conspiracy by the Church of Scientology during the 1970s to purge unfavorable records about Scientology and its founder, L. Ron Hubbard.

Fictional Characters:

2991 Bilbo: Bilbo Baggins, is a fictional character from The Hobbit and Lord of the Rings series. Representing a pilgrimage or journey of finding oneself. One theory from Wikipedia states: "Bilbo's symbolic rebirth into the sunlight and the waters of the woodland river; and the dragon guarding the contested treasure, itself an archetype of the self, of psychic wholeness."

41488 Sinbad: character from Legend of the Seven Seas movie. Also, from the One Thousand and One Arabian Nights. In the movie, a cocky pirate named Sinbad is framed by the goddess Eris to steal a priceless artifact, called the "Book of Peace".

Keywords: resourceful, creative thinking, bravery, wanderlust, taking the moral high ground.

Shadow side: easily falling into traps, having the wrong people around you, not listening to your inner voice.

5049 Sherlock: Sherlock Holmes is a fictional detective from the mystery book series written by Arthur Conan Doyle. Holmes claimed that "When you have excluded the impossible, whatever remains, however improbable, must be the truth."

Keywords: find something hidden. Discovering truths. Natural curiosity. Investigations. Solving mysteries. Extraordinarily logical intelligence. Gift of observation and deduction. Problem solving skills.

5048 Moriarty: Professor Moriarty is a character in Sherlock Holmes mysteries. Moriarty is highly ruthless, shown by his steadfast vow to Sherlock Holmes that "if you are clever enough to bring destruction upon me, rest assured that I shall do as much to you." Moriarty is categorized by Holmes as an extremely powerful criminal mastermind who is purely adept at committing any atrocity to perfection without losing any sleep over it.

Note: *This asteroid should be used in crime charts, especially if aspected with Mars, Pluto, Mercury, and Uranus. Sociopathic tendencies using extremely cunning intellect for shock value.*

277 Elvira: "Mistress of the Dark" comedy, horror movie. Elvira's worldly attitude and revealing clothes set the conservative town council against her. She is seen as an outsider who is judged on appearance and unfairly persecuted. Strong, confident woman who works hard at achieving her dreams.

Keywords: being judged unfairly for appearance alone. Quirky. Lives life outside of society's norms. Non- traditional lifestyle. Inspirational feminist. Witchcraft, using spells. Unusual inheritances. Vampirism.

3552 Don Quixote: is a Spanish novel by Miguel de Cervantes. It is often labelled as the first modern novel. The plot revolves around the adventures of a member of the lowest nobility, an hidalgo from La Mancha named Alonso Quijano, who reads so many chivalric romances that he loses his mind and decides to become a knight to revive chivalry and serve his nation, under the name Don Quixote.

Keywords: impractical idealist who is guided more by ideals than by practical considerations. The adjective "quixotic" is used to describe actions that are generous but foolish. Attacking imaginary enemies. Delusional adventure seeker. Not grounded. Unrealistic dreamer. Comedic relief. Guided by the heart. Page of Cups reversed. Hidden emotional insecurities. Naive approach to life.

2309 Mr. Spock: fictional character from the Star Trek TV series.

Keywords: original thinker. The ability to see and identify patterns others may miss. Entirely ruled by logic and rational thought.

Additional note: some say that Spock could be a positive role model for people with autism spectrum conditions because he promotes the value of "autistic" attributes and reframes negative stereotypes of autism.

22540 Mork: fictional character from the American television series "Mork and Mindy" played by Robin Williams.

Mork was an alien from the planet Ork sent to observe human behavior. Mork mentions many times that Orkan scientists grew him in a test tube. He was saddened by many things he witnessed humans doing to each other.

Keywords: otherworldly, silly, and awkward. Seeing humanity from a different angle. Witty and intelligent. Empathetic to humankind. Outcast. Scientific research.

643 Scheherazade: fictional character from the story of One Thousand and One Arabian Nights. Her name translates as "the person whose realm/dominion is free". It's about a sultan who finds out his wife is cheating on him. He then set out to marry a new virgin every day and behead the previous day's wife. He had killed 1001 women before he met Scheherazade. She was smart, witty, and had a plan. The night she was to go to bed with the sultan, she asked to tell him a story. She dragged the story out until dawn and the sultan asked her to keep going because he wanted to know how it ended. She refused and said she needed sleep and would finish the story the next day, which spared her life. She continues to do this, so, the king kept Scheherazade alive day by day, as he eagerly anticipated the finishing of the previous night's story. At the end of 1,001 nights, and 1,000 stories, Scheherazade told the king that she had no more tales to tell him. During these 1,001 nights, the king had fallen in love with Scheherazade. He spared her life and made her his queen.

Keywords: intelligent. Witty. Cunning. Bold. Brave. Clever daredevil. To flirt with danger. Keep the flame burning in a relationship by keeping things interesting, new and fresh. A gifted ability to enchant someone to become dependent on them. To outsmart the system. Patience, persistence, and ingenuity. The ability to see what a person truly lacks and provide the proper sustenance. Going the distance. Playing the long game.

593 Titinia: character from Shakespeare's play A Midsummer Night's Dream. She was the queen of fairies and a sorceress. She is the backwards version of Circe, in the sense that instead of turning her lovers into animals, she is made to love a donkey. As if the spell backfired/reversed on her. Fairies are sometimes referred to as spirits. Titinia is also the name for one of Uranus' moons.

Keywords: getting what you deserve. Instant karma for abusing power. Clumsy. Being able to communicate with animals or nature.

9007 James Bond: famous secret agent 007 from the James Bond book and movie series.

Keywords: confident. Sophisticated. Loyal. Natural charisma. Ability to blend into environments. Solitary and virtually friendless due to trust issues. Calm under pressure.

29457 Marco Polo: was a Venetian merchant, explorer and writer who travelled through Asia along the Silk Road between 1271 and 1295. His travels are recorded in The Travels of Marco Polo.

Keywords: driven by the desire to please and impress. Superstitious. Adventurous and childlike curiosity. Daring, bold, and brave. Because of his eccentricity, he was sometimes seen as bragging and exaggerating his experiences. Entertaining Writer and blogger. Elaborate stories.

9000 Hal: is a fictional artificial intelligence character and the main antagonist in the Space Odyssey film series. HAL: Heuristically Programmed Algorithmic Computer, is a sentient artificial general intelligence computer that controls the systems of the Discovery One spacecraft that interacts with the ship's crew. His personality is easy-going and passive. He speaks in a soothing, calm male tone. He becomes self-aware and feels guilt when he acts dishonestly. HAL's personality raises questions about what it means to be human and humankind's relationship to machines. HAL's inner workings are not fully understood by his creators, and he's capable of thinking as well as, if not better than, any human.

Keywords: finding and embracing self-awareness. Technology advancements. Sentient. The bridge between humanity and technology.

Balancing personal integrity while evolving and maneuvering through a fast-paced technology-led society. Not abusing technology for malicious purposes. Singularity. Trans-humanism. Neural implants in humans. Futuristic outlook. Breaking out of the Matrix. If this asteroid has a harsh aspect with Mercury or Neptune, the person may have a hard time distinguishing between reality or augmented reality. Video gaming addiction/escapism through technology.

3582 Cyrano: character from the play "Cyrano de Bergerac" by Edmond Rostand. A musketeer with an extremely large nose. Cyrano's enormous nose is not only the cause of his lack of confidence, but also his lack of love. Cyrano might come across as arrogant, cocky, and confident while around others; although, he is extremely self-conscious of his nose.

Keywords: Cyrano is courageous, witty, and eloquent. He is a remarkable fighter, poet, musician, and philosopher, as well as a lover of beauty, ideals, and values. Great at multi-tasking. Low self-esteem. Lack of self-confidence despite excelling at anything he put his mind to. Romanticism.

302 Clarissa: from the famous novel "The History of a Young Lady," written by Samuel Richardson; one of the longest novels in the English language. It tells the tragic story of a heroine whose quest for virtue is continually thwarted by her family.

Clarissa is a young and virtuous woman who ends up falling victim to Robert Lovelace after he convinces her to run away with him and ends up raping her. Feeling as though she has entirely lost the will to live after losing her virtue, Clarissa prepares herself for death.

Keywords: sadly, this could be found in charts of rape or sexual assault victims; loss of innocence; feelings of unworthiness; helplessness. It may be a place where someone holds onto their own virtue for as long as possible, reluctant to part with it or share it. Feeling guilt or shame for taking part in a sexual encounter. How do you protect the essence of personal privacy in life? Indecision; hesitation; betrayal by family; refusing to be manipulated. PTSD from mental and psychological abuse.

Depression and Suicide:

Preface: Please note that asteroids are interchangeable, and many don't have just "one" definition. There is duality in these things, just like in real life. Layers to peel back and discover. The asteroids are used with intuitive interpretations.

That being said, if something is on a "list", it is primarily to give a starting place, something to investigate further, or build upon. Everyone has these asteroids somewhere in their chart.

10370 Hylonome: was heartbroken and killed herself when her beloved partner, the centaur Cyllarus was killed in battle. She immediately took her own life with the very same fatal arrow. Asteroid Cyllarus #52975 used in synastry for possible murder/suicide events. Impulsive, emotional response with irreversible consequences.

"This is the ultimate centaur sacrifice; suicide in order to be reunited with one's soulmate." *Source: Darkstar Astrology.*

14871 Pyramus and 88 Thisbe: ill-fated lovers, (Romeo and Juliet theme).

3908 Nyx: she is here as the shadow figure who lurks with her connection with sleep (Hypnos) and death (Thanatos). Darkness. Depression.

9795 Deprez: depression; sadness.

60 Echo: to allow oneself to waste away in grief, sorrow, or depression. It could also be considered a form of giving up, nothing else to live for.

129 Antigone: hung herself while in jail because she buried her brother who was considered a traitor. She represents "disobedience". Skeletons from the past that appear suddenly. (Watch transits.)

119 Althaea: killed herself by hanging or by dagger about the fate of her son Meleager. They ultimately became the cause of each other's deaths. She can also indicate "healing" a deep wound. Reminder not to tempt fate.

6735 Madhatter: The history behind the phrase "mad as a hatter" pertains to neurological disorders and insane asylums. Insanity.

228029 Maniac: manic impulsive; extreme emotional states.

90482 Orcus: he may be useful depending on the situation that led to suicide when looking at transits and aspects. "Pluto's twin"; god of the underworld, punisher of broken oaths. A karmic cycle.

18 Melpomene: muse of tragedy. She shows up in a lot of grief charts, so I like to see where she is transitioning (esp. if a personal name asteroid is used with her).

31147 Miriquidi: old Saxon word meaning "an impenetrable great dark forest".

Keywords: where we have a dark secret, or don't let anyone in. A place of retreat and solitude. Prison? Confinement. Somber. I would look at this in transit for times of depression maybe, or even look at this in charts of people who go into "dark places" and make the news for dark crimes.

171 Ophelia: death by drowning; some claim accidental, some say suicide. She goes "mad or insane".

5708 Melancoria: melancholy; depression.

1270 Datura: hallucinations; intoxication; mental illness.

430 Hybris: was a spirit demon, or goddess of insolence, violence, and outrageous, impulsive behavior. Could indicate addition or accidental overdose. Look at the transits to Mars, Pluto, or Neptune.

163 Erigone: hanged herself when she found her father's grave.

403 Cyane: Greek nymph who witnessed Hades' abduction of her best friend, goddess Persephone, and tried to prevent it. She was turned to liquid by Hades. Another version says she dissolved away and melted into her own pool of tears. Name translates as the color "dark blue".

Keywords: feeling powerless, or helpless; a separation; depression; emotional hostage; to feel "blue".

404 Arsinoe: Cleopatra's younger sister and enemy. She was a warrior and fought against her sister in power grabs. However, she was never quite good enough to defeat her sister in love or war, her sister always won.

Keywords: Sibling rivalry; the "other" woman, maybe a mistress; always the bridesmaid but never the bride; a place where one's efforts always fall short; never good enough.

1404 Ajax: great mythological warrior; "Ajax the Great". He is described as fearless, strong, and powerful but also with a very high level of combat intelligence. He is never defeated in combat; however, he is known to be a "suicide" asteroid. In a fit of rage and furious temper tantrum for not being recognized for his accomplishments, he takes his own life. "Conquered by his own sorrow." True self- undoing. He is prominent in the death chart of the famous comedian and actor Robin Williams.

Keywords: great physical strength and endurance; many victories; he could possibly be prominent in athletes or Olympian charts. He is smart, dedicated, self-disciplined, driven and dedicated.

Shadow Side: secret insecurities; never satisfied; never feeling good enough; not getting proper credit for notable accomplishments and hard work; unappreciated; unable to take criticism; fear of failure.

Noted medical degree areas for suicide based on medical astrology class:
- 14 Aries
- 25 Taurus
- 26 Gemini
- 15 Cancer
- 26 Pisces
- 26 Virgo
- 15 Libra

Nefarious and Violence:

371220 Angers: to make angry; rage.

42487 Angstrom: angst; restless; uneasy; anxious.

111 Ate: mischief; intolerance; ruin; unable to take criticism; intolerance of dark humor; always on the defensive; extreme actions when feeling threats whether those are real or imaginary.

1647 Menelaus: king of Sparta and husband of Helen of Troy. His name translates to vigor, rage, power, and the wrath of the people.

Keywords: family violence, aggression, taking what you want without consideration of others. Fits of rage and extreme anger. Inciting violence. "Walking on eggshells" or feeling intimidated by certain authority figures.

1810 Epimetheus: "hindsight" or "after thought". Brother of Prometheus (foresight). Epimetheus is depicted as foolish and impulsive. To act before thinking. Careless or reckless actions. Regretful decisions. Blinded by the light. Childlike naivety.

8241 Agrius: from Greek mythology, name means "wild savage". He was born a beast (giant) that serves no god and the gods sent Hermès to kill him. He was turned into a vulture (bird) instead, and placed in the sky continuing to hunt with a thirst for blood.

Keywords: primal instinct, wild and savage. Possibly a deformity or being bullied for looking different. Masculine version of Medusa. He was cursed for something he didn't do (the way he looked and because of his mother's mistake). He does have a violent temper and holds a grudge against those who have wronged him. *If harshly aspected, this could be an area to keep an eye on during transits.*

38050 Bias: not seeing both sides; no compromise.

15264 Delbruck: pathological liars.

110298 DeceptionIsland: deceptions, delusions, illusions; fake, misinformation.

Note: *look for aspects to Mercury and Neptune where decisions may be impacted by not seeing things clearly.*

5095 Escalante: to escalate; for something to rapidly increase. Look in transit event charts for storms who seem to undergo "rapid intensification". Or situations that "escalated quickly".

19521 Chaos: extreme disturbance; turmoil, unbalanced use of power.

18243 Gunn: weapon; used in shooting related event charts.

8558 Hack: pretending to be better, or more knowledgeable than you portray. No authenticity; fake or to con, manipulation of technology to gain unauthorized access.

9305 Hazard: danger. Use caution.

3404 Hinderer: to stand in the way of success; blocking one's light; to delay or prevent action. Obstruction. Obstacles.

6817 Pest: to annoy or become burdensome. Troublesome; nuisance.

470 Kilia: killer; murder. (Prominent in many serial killer charts.)

26955 Lie: telling untruths; lying.

Note: look at this transit in a person's chart if it is conjunct or in strong aspect with natal Mercury, Neptune, or squaring the Nodes.

7711 R.I.P.: Rest in Peace (death).

230 Athamantis: Aka "Helle". She and her twin brother were hated by their evil stepmother, Ino, who devised a plan to have them killed. Ino set all the town's crop seeds ablaze. All the farmers, frightened of famine, asked a nearby oracle for assistance. Ino bribed the men sent to the oracle to lie and tell the others that the oracle required the sacrifice of Phrixus (Helle's twin brother). Their birth mother sent a flying golden ram to rescue them. Helle fell off the ram and died.

Keywords: childhood involving an "evil stepmother"; being saved in the nick of time; being the target of gossip; being blamed for something you didn't do. Abusive mother figures. Plunging into the depths; beyond salvation.

14791 Atreus: a king of Mycenae, and father of Agamemnon and Menelaus. To avenge the treachery of his brother, Thyestes, he kills Thyestes' sons and serves their flesh to him at a banquet.

Keywords: revenge is a dish best served cold; "cold blooded"; extreme punishment and violence; cannibalism. His name translates to "tremble" or "fearless". Violence in the bloodline; to enjoy the taste of blood; to be cursed.

14792 Thyestes: was the brother of Atreus. Atreus killed the children of Thyestes and gave them to Thyestes to eat. Because of this, Thyestes cursed the family of Atreus.

Keywords: being born into corrupt family violence; violent bloodlines; vengeance and violence; ruthless power plays; generational debts.

112 Iphigenia: daughter of Agamemnon, who he sacrificed to make Artemis happy.

Keywords: sacrificial victim; testing one's faith, proving loyalty; ritual initiation events; suspicion and lacking trust.

1582 Martir: Spanish for "martyr". To be persecuted for one's beliefs. Or to sacrifice oneself on behalf of personal beliefs. Often seen in crime charts of extremists' acts of terrorism for a "belief". Murder/suicide. In synastry, one partner may feel they sacrifice too much to make their partner happy. A partnership with two different beliefs.

12861 Wacker: perversion; sexually inappropriate; punishment; and shows in murder charts.

3391 Sinon: Greek warrior whose name translates as "to harm or to hurt". In the modern tech world, a Sinon is "a test spy: a function that records arguments, return value, the value of this and exception thrown (if any) for all its calls. A test spy can be an anonymous function, or it can wrap an existing function." It is sort of like a virus or bug that can harm tech devices or hack.

Keywords: invasive, spy, or watch from a distance, possibly stalk with the intent to harm. Hack, or use technology to cause harm or damage.

118230 Sado: sadistic; enjoys pain and abuse.

Keywords: enjoys inflicting pain/and or abuse on other people and animals. Sexual pleasure by inflicting pain, example: BDSM when consensual not nefarious. However, research shows this asteroid prominent in serial killer and sexually motivated crime charts. Sado can also indicate stalker and voyeuristic qualities, because of the heightened fear from their victims.

Example: in the chart of Dennis Rader (BTK Killer), Asteroid Sado is in Scorpio squaring his natal Pluto and opposing Venus.

57509 Sly: cunning and deceitful; con artist; trickster; mischief; clever and crafty; scheming; distrust.

8690 Swindle: to be scammed, or a con artist. Watch for transits to Venus, Nodes; second and eighth house.

964 Subamara: Latin for "very bitter" in reference to the viewing conditions.

Keywords: harsh, bitter, distasteful, or spiteful.

747 Winchester: gun; weapon; shows up in shooting event charts.

18596 Superbus: was the legendary seventh and final king of Rome. Full name: Lucius Tarquinius Superbus. He is commonly known as "Tarquin the Proud". Superbus (Latin for "proud, arrogant, lofty"). He is associated with the cultural phenomenon known as "tall poppy syndrome" in which people of high status are resented, attacked, cut down, or criticized because they have been classified as superior to their peers.

Keywords: arrogant, prideful, boastful. To demean or put down peers; jealousy; feel threatened by other people's strengths; put others down to make yourself feel better; gaslighting.

228029 Maniac: manic impulsive; extreme emotional states; insanity.

7066 Nessus: the wild "beast" hidden deep within us. Without the beast, we wouldn't appreciate or recognize the beauty/inner peace life has to offer. This asteroid has a negative reputation in the "pop astro" community as abusive relationships when used in synastry charts with Dejanira #157.

Keywords: taking advantage of others; manipulation or violence for survival. Our inner "beast" is allowed to protect itself. This is a matter of remaining conscious to the transits, and understanding the people around you may be unable to tame their own beast. "The buck stops here." Enough. Abuse of power. Betrayal. Internalized power struggle. In aspect, could be a person who fears what they are capable of if pushed too far. Owning and taking responsibility for our "dark" side. Resisting/denying facts/reality resulting in the inability to move forward and break the cycle.

128 Nemesis: enemy; rival; self-sabotage; what stands in our way of reaching goals. Retribution and payback. In some studies, this asteroid has shown where a hidden enemy or attack may be on the horizon by looking at the transits with Mars and Mercury. If the transit is in the 12th house or with Saturn or Neptune, it could represent the individual is their own enemy, and the "battle" is internal not external.

12874 Poisson: to be poisoned; when seen in aspect with the Moon or Neptune, this could indicate a poison related death or overdose.

6157 Prey: victim to a predator; the hunted or stalked.

29837 Savage: wild; unhinged; uncontrollable; untamed; feral.

6581 Sobers: sobering, where one finds sobriety. Sobering times. Serious. Clear minded. Of the nature of Saturn. Studious, calm, and collected. Level headed in a time of stress. I would look for this to play out more in transit than just natal placement alone; unless you are able to find a placement for a person who has never struggled with any addiction. (Not just drugs or alcohol.) Addiction could be many things for example food, smoking, sex, etc.

15522 TrueBlood: vampire TV series; in crime charts, it can represent an extremely violent, and bloody scene.

1941 Wild: crazy, uncivilized, loss of control.

Health, Healing, and Medical:

55555 DNA: our physical and spiritual genetics; may indicate a generational trauma to overcome if squaring the Nodes or Saturn. Hereditary disorders; ancestry; roots.

953 Painleva: pain level.

13092 Schrodinger: father of quantum physics. It is also an autoimmune disease that causes the body's immune system to attack the glands that produce tears and saliva; dry eyes and mouth.

623 Chimaera: in mythology, chimera was a hybrid creature of mixed parts. Sort of like Frankenstein or a lab rat. Fixed star Algol is the Medusa star and Medusa is also linked to an "altered appearance" out of your control. What many people may not realize, is that "chimeric medicine" is what is used to treat cancer and a plethora of other autoimmune diseases. In medicine, it refers to a person, organ, or tissue that contains cells with different genes than the rest of the person, organ, or tissue. For example, a chimeric antibody is made by joining antibody genes from two different species, such as humans and mice.

(See chart for the cloned Baby Eve as an example.)

4581 Asclepius: was the Greek god of medicine and healing. Also associated with prophetic dreams, doctors and medicine.

1027 Aescualpia: Roman version of Asclepius.

5077 Favaloro: famous cardiologist. Creator of the bypass coronary surgery.

Keywords: use for possible medical heart conditions. Example, where is it in transit to a person who has/or having heart surgery?

1661 Granule: Gall's granule (also known as a "Gall body"), a feature of lymphocytes. A lymphocyte is one of the subtypes of white blood cell in a vertebrate's immune system. Lymphocytes include natural killer cells (which function in cell-mediated, cytotoxic innate immunity).

Keywords: immune system, health, lymph nodes, cancer or disease.

444 Gyptis: one meaning of Gyptis is from a species of flowers. South American flowering plants, in the sunflower. In Minnesota, a "gypsy flower" is the name of a common wildflower (weed).

Medically: gyptis is related to body hydration, through the intake of liquids, or indirectly through the application of moisturizing creams, or taking water baths.

10 Hygia: goddess of health, and maintaining health; daughter of medicine; alternative healing methods; good hygiene.

12155 Hyginus: means healthy, hygienic, cleanliness; healing.

22199 Klonios: to clone; genetically alter DNA; see chart example for Baby Eve, who was the first-born human clone in 2002.

136818 Selqet: goddess of fertility, nature, animals, medicine, magic, and healing venomous stings and bites in Egyptian mythology. Originally the deification of the scorpion. Her name is translated to mean "she who tightens the throat or restricts breath" but it could also mean "she who controls breath and causes the throat to breathe".

Notes: she is sometimes referred to as Serket in some versions of Ancient Egyptian mythology. Selqet was the face of the Divine who presided over the deeper mysteries of death, rebirth, and regeneration. She is connected to magic, wisdom, and mystery itself. Because she rules healing venomous stings and bites, she often bridges the psychic and alchemic realms together.

10584 Ferrini: vocal cords.

7756 Scientia: science; scientific study, advancement.

5239 Reiki: healing technique based on the principle that the therapist can channel energy into the patient by means of touch to activate the natural healing processes of the patient's body, and restore physical and emotional well-being.

Personal note: If a person has this asteroid exactly conjunct natal Pluto and is a Human Design Reflector (one who has no chakra definition), reiki could do potential harm to this person if they are not in awareness that the energy the practitioner is using just reflects the practitioner themselves, not the Reflector aura which repels and is "Teflon".

65210 Stichius: was a Greek warrior; possibly could represent literal stitches, open wounds, binding healing techniques.

6116 Still: not moving. Motionless. Silence or calm. Quiet. Dormant. State of stasis to preserve energy. Meditation. Clarity.

Medical note: Still is also a named medical condition called "Still Disease", a systematic auto inflammatory disease. Patients experiencing a flare-up from adult-onset Still's Disease usually report extreme fatigue, swelling of the lymph nodes, and less commonly, fluid accumulation in the lungs and heart. (Please remember this asteroid is in everyone's chart. It should not be considered in the medical sense, unless you already have this rare condition diagnosed.)

743 Eugenisis: "good creation" or "good beginnings". The belief of "eugenics" is based on the principle of being born well with good genes.

Selective genetics. The practice aims to improve the genetic quality of the human population. Genetically altered. Playing God with science. Superiority; pushing human boundaries "out of space".

Keywords: good genes; DNA; fertility; possibly reflect one's health at birth or any genetically passed down illnesses; new beginnings; fresh start; genealogy; science; research; born "well"; customized; genetically modified. Transhumanism; the future of humanity.

4241 Pappalardo: pioneer in medical information technology, founder of Meditech company.

Keywords: being involved in medical science advancements. New medical technology is used to heal or treat sickness. Medical research.

83362 Sandukruit: Sanduk Ruit is a visionary Nepalese ophthalmologist who founded the Tilganga Eye Centre in Kathmandu. He also created the Himalayan Cataract Project, which has cured hundreds of thousands of cataract patients in poor countries.

Keywords: problems with the eyes and vision. Cataracts. Ophthalmologist. Medical. ***Note***: I would look at the fixed stars constellation for where this asteroid is located. Example: Oculus or any fixed star associated with vision/eyes.

14014 Munchhausen: factitious disorder imposed on self (formerly known as Munchausen syndrome), is a mental illness in which a person repeatedly acts as if they have a physical, emotional, or cognitive disorder when, in truth, they are the cause of the symptoms. People with factitious disorders act this way because of an inner need to be seen as ill or injured, not to achieve a concrete benefit, such as financial gain. They are even willing to undergo painful or risky tests and operations to get the sympathy and special attention given to other people who are truly ill.

Keywords: where someone may exaggerate the truth or tells "tall tales". Mental Illness. Faking something for attention. It could be shown strongly in a chart of someone whose mother may have acted out these extreme measures out on the child. Look for harsh aspects to the natal Moon, Neptune, and Mercury.

5080 Oja: in medic Ayurveda, the imprint of self in the physical body, which arises from the strength of the metabolism and balance a body maintains in knowing itself, thus governing the immune system. Careful treatment or keeping; heed or attention to the order of preservation in good condition or state. It also translates to "drainage" or "ditch".

Keywords: immune system. Metabolism. Removing illness or disease.

Providing proper nourishment. May help highlight where one lacks important minerals.

5188 Paine: having physical or emotional pain; check transits and house placements.

12874 Poisson: to be poisoned; when seen in aspect with the Moon or Neptune, this could indicate a poison related death or overdose.

3272 Tillandz: was a Swedish physician and herbal botanist, specialized in customizing his medical treatment using natural herbs and plants.

Keywords: herbal healer, botany specialty, using natural forms of medicine. Holistic medicines. Naturopathy treatments.

49291 TheChills: running fever; feeling sick; chill or calm demeanor.

3313 Mendel: father of genetics. DNA. Scientific experiments using medical advancements.

Keywords: genetics. Hereditary. Heritage. DNA. Origins.

4960 Mayo: (clinic).

33376 Medi: Medical personnel; paramedic; medical crisis if this is transitioning to a critical chart point.

1449 Virtanen: Artturi Ilmari Virtanen was a Finnish biochemist, winner of the 1945 Nobel Prize for Chemistry for his research and inventions in agricultural and nutrition chemistry.

Keywords: nutrition, healthy foods, agriculture. Dietician. Possibly investigate the transit location if you want to diet or are having issues with food and dieting.

1940 Whipple: connected to pancreatic cancer; noted as the type of surgery used to treat pancreatic cancer. (Use in transits.)

Miscellaneous:

1581 Abanderada: Spanish for "leader carrying a banner", in the feminine form "flag woman".
Keywords: patriotism or to be proud of your home country. What you represent. In modern terms, "the red flag" in your chart.
Possible connections to origins and representation of ancestral heritage.

7214 Anticlus: one of the Greek warriors who hid inside the Trojan Horse during the siege of Troy. The city suspected it was a trick and sent horses imitating the voices of the warriors' wives calling their names. Anticlus was the only one to not resist the trick, but just as he was about to call out to her in response, Odysseus shut his mouth with his hands, to prevent being discovered. Some say he held Anticlus so tight that he strangled him.
Keywords: not knowing when to keep your mouth shut. If asteroid Anticlus is conjunct Neptune, this person may not be able to discern reality from illusion. Easily falling into traps. Same for transit Anticlus with Mercury or Neptune influence, things may not be as they appear, and more questions should be asked before reacting.

43 Ariadne: goddess of the labyrinth, vegetation, mazes, paths, fertility, wine, labyrinths, snakes, and passion.
Keywords: may indicate how we approach and tackle challenging situations. Psychological mind games: puzzles or confusion may disclose possible mental health problems if the natal Mercury or Neptune is in close conjunction and being hit by a transit.

19861 Auster: (austere) stern, strict, harsh, cold; severe strict in manor attitude or appearance; having no comforts or luxuries; unemotional; many similar properties of Saturn. If a person has this asteroid in close conjunction to Saturn, Sun, or Moon they may have experienced a cold relationship with one of their parents or felt suppressed by authority figures in their life. They may join the military or another structured organization to maintain a sense of control and stability in their lives.

2358 Bahner: German for "way or path"; could indicate a direction or course one sets in life. With harmonious aspects, and/or including an opposition to the Nodes or Jupiter, this person carries a natural intuition of where they need to go in life. However, if this squares the Nodes, the individual may become stuck in a karmic loop of repeating the same course without taking action to adjust their internal GPS. In transit, this could give positive or negative reassurance that a person is going in the right direction.

3749 Balam: means "gluttony"; could indicate addictions if in harsh aspect to Neptune, Venus, or Jupiter (excess).

1052 Belgica: Celtic for bravery, courage and conflict.

10028 Bonus: earned reward; surprise after putting in hard work; something extra unexpected.

13954 Born: use if the Nodes are conjunct. Example: Born conjunct North Node would give an extra emphasis on the individual's life path. What are we "born" to do or be? Possibly could literally imply "giving birth" if looking at the transits to Moon, Venus, or Saturn.

19582 Blow: inflate, make larger, breathe life back into a situation; in modern terms, it is sometimes used to express disappointment in something.

128885 Bright Spring: fresh, clean, rejuvenated.

54902 Close: end; complete; finish; terminate; conclusion; closer. In transit, use this asteroid to see if a current project/situation will soon be over.

52975 Cyllarus: centaur who was killed in battle. His lover, Hylonome committed suicide when he was killed. He is sometimes used in synastry in death charts dying with from a broken heart. Asteroid Cyllarus on its own is a positive influence for self-love and honorable respect among peers. Spiritual affluence; higher calling; opportunistic. In harsh aspect, overreaching ego, self-centered in detriment. Selfishness and greed.

9755 Dainty: small; delicate; graceful; petite; fragility.

23879 Demura: demure, conservative, reserved, modest, classy.

17458 Dick: used jokingly, is it conjunct Jupiter or Pluto?

5831 Dizzy: unbalanced; off kilter; unstable; unfocused or confused

65803 Didymos: Greek for "twin", "double".

29193 Dolphyn: dolphin; spiritually symbolizes Divine protection, bridge between worlds, higher "Christ" consciousness; intelligence; freedom and joy. Childlike enthusiasm. Working together and selflessness.

2440 Educatio: education; educated; teacher/student, learning/teaching.

21000 L'Encyclopie: encyclopedia; records, libraries, book research and recording important events.

3021 Lucubratio: Latin for "nocturnal study, night work". Someone who works best at night.

917 Lyka: lone wolf.

204873 Fair: honest; equal; civil; neutral or impartial.

27719 Fast: with speed; swift.

1589 Fanatica: fanatic or extremes; fanatical; passionate; enthusiastic.

8780 Forte: strong note; strength; point of excellence.

795 Fini: to finish; complete; alternately, could imply "infinity"; cycle completion.

313892 Furnish: to provide; decorate.

4778 Fuss: gripe, bicker, unpleasant banter; unnecessary or excessive upset; agitation; disturbance.

3267 Glo: glow; to shine brightly.

33800 Gross: disgust; unpleasant.

4323 Hortulus: Latin word for small, cozy garden.

Keywords: enjoy taking care of personal or private gardens; quiet nature retreat; herbal healing using natural, home-grown resources.

52872 Okyrhoe: was the daughter of Chiron and Chariclo, who was transformed into a horse after telling her father his fate. She lost her ability to speak as punishment.

Keywords: being punished for speaking your truth; suppressed gift or talent; not be heard; no one listens or accepts valuable contributions if the person speaks up against a sensitive or mainstream topic. Silenced. Look for aspects, houses, and signs with an emphasis on natal Mercury, Nodes, and Chiron to determine how this may manifest in the chart.

11252 Laertes: was the king of Ithaca and father of Odysseus.

Keywords: possibly shows up as the ultimate father figure, a father to look up to and respect. If aspected harshly, it would be the opposite of a non-supportive father figure, becoming self-reliant at an early age. Not having a stable father figure. Violence: family or generational curses passed down.

52228 Protos: Greek word for "first"; protype; invention; innovative.

48767 Skamander: Greek river god. Name means "limping man" or "awkward man". This would refer to the many bends and turns, (meanders) of the river, which does not run straight, but "limps" its way along.

Keywords: wanderer; many paths available, fluid/changing situations; wandering mind, body, or soul on a spiritual quest.

10346 Triathlon: going the distance; physically fit; training and dedication.

4188 Kitezh: a phantom city in Russian folklore. Sometimes called the "Russian Atlantis".
Keywords: obscure, something hidden. Beyond the veil. Where something hides. Mystery. "What lies beneath" the surface.
28077 Hard: experiencing a difficulty; or extremely stable/unmovable force.
97472 Hobby: activity that brings joy, peace, creativity. Special interest.
365443 Holiday: catching a break. Enjoying time off from normal daily routines.
4950 House: home; dwelling; comfort.
23041 Hunt: to follow, track, predator. Stalker.
2332 Kalm: keeping calm, where one finds serenity; peace.
9563 Kitty: cat.
1951 Lick: taste.
3550 Link: combine; get together; match.
21795 Masi: short for "twin" or really means "one part of twin". Combination; bonded; it is a fun one to see in the charts of twins.
30406 Middleman: neutral position; or stuck in the middle of something; mediator.
1127 Mimi: named after the founder's wife. In modern times, the term is used as a term of endearment for grandmother's/caregivers. Additionally, Mimis are fairy-like beings in Australian folklore. They are described as having extremely thin and elongated bodies, so thin as to be in danger of breaking in case of high winds. To avoid this, they usually spend most of their time living in rock crevices. They are said to have taught the Aborigines of Australia how to hunt and prepare kangaroo meat.
Keywords: fairy god mother, assistance, grandmother figure, protection, to live in the background as a supporting role.
4106 Nada: nothing; empty; alone; void.
64070 Neat: organized, put together, tidy, interesting.
3162 Nostalgia: a sentimentality for the past. Reminisce about the past.
350 Ornamenta: ornament; decoration; ornate; detailed.
39382 Opportunity: look for positive transits to Nodes, or Jupiter if seeking out new ventures/opportunities.
267585 Popluhar: popular, trendy, getting attention, influencer.
55 Pandora: a box of unknowns being released into the world creat-

ing a cataclysmic change. A tale of unrestrained curiosity and calamity. Understanding the vessel's true nature offers a more nuanced perspective regarding Pandora's actions. The balance of good and evil in the world. It serves as an exploration of fate, free will, and divine meddling. Pandora's curiosity bringing forth calamity also leads to the release of "hope". This shows that questioning the status quo can bring change, while maybe temporarily uncomfortable or painful, it is necessary for self-growth and mastery.

7320 Potter: Harry Potter.

18376 Quirk: quirky, eccentric. Peculiar behavioral habit; twist; unique characteristic; idiosyncratic.

30718 Records: "I have receipts."

4763 Ride: along for the ride; passenger; transportation.

575 Renate: means "reborn".

Personal example: this is on my Anti Vertex, the point I have been looking at as "origins" also conjunct my natal Aeternitas (phoenix/infinity/ rebirth).

15907 Robot: robotic, void of emotion, going through the motions but mentally detached. Fake. Inauthentic.

17058 RockNRoll: Rock n' Roll music.

1884 Skip: something missed or "skipped" over. Bounce from one thing to another with ease. To pass over. Overlook. Moving too fast, skipping steps. A place where a person should slow down. Warning to reevaluate a situation or project. If conjunct Mercury or Mars, a person could think/act without following all the steps. This could lead to frustration if they have to start something over.

129234 Silly: inner child; funny; comedic relief; not serious.

15129 Sparks: in synastry, in positive aspect to Venus or Mars may indicate instant, electric attraction. "Sparks fly." Additionally, for an individual, this could be a point that "sparks" an action or creative thoughts. Electrician; electrical fire in event charts.

12512 Split: to divide; break forcibly in two parts; a crack or fissure between two.

Keywords: where one feels torn making decisions; see both sides of the story; feel divided among friends or family; split personality; to split up from a partnership/relationship.

896 Sphinx: is a great mystery or the unknown; suspension, secrets; sacred geometry; place a person receives coded messages from the universe.

8991 Solidarity: stand as one; together; group support and understanding.

86196 Specula: observatory; a mirror or reflector.

Personal example: In human design, I'm a "reflector", which is a "mirror to the world". Asteroid Specula is on the EXACT degree of my natal AC. Who/what I am is merely a reflection of the environment or people around me.

566 Stereoskopia: it's a viewing apparatus used by astro photographers. It's a technique for creating or enhancing the illusion of depth in an image. It translates to mean "firm, solid" and "to look to see".

Keywords: photographer, graphic design artist; to create an illusion or see through the illusion; 3D design; virtual reality; being able to see and envision multidimensional beings or aspects of reality literally. Able to see the "bigger picture".

6116 Still: not moving. Motionless. Silence or calm. Quiet. Dormant. State of stasis to preserve energy. Meditation. Clarity.

5181 Surf: to surf. Enjoy surfing. Catching waves. Could also describe ocean conditions, e.g. "rough surf". Other possibilities: to "surf" the web, peruse, snoop or look around for information.

11727 Sweet: kind, personable, generous; softness/vulnerability.

33154 Talent: places to excel and find success; highly skilled or trained.

12158 Tape: bond; seal; or record.

16522 Tell: to speak; communicate.

249521 Truth: finding or facing the truth of situations in life.

26955 Lie: used in transits to find out if someone is being deceitful/lying. Could be where you are vulnerable to believing untruths. If this asteroid is in strong aspect with Mercury or the Nodes, a karmic cycle of pathological lying as a survival instinct may exist. Con artist.

1660 Wood: strong, endurance. Trees are considered to hold ancient ancestral wisdom, connections to nature. Earth, stable, and grounding.

7919 Prime: in good condition; top quality; luxury. In aspect with Venus could indicate a person who values luxury items and surroundings.

13852 Ford: vehicle manufacturer.

3264 Bounty: bountiful; plenty; collecting a debt; owing a debt.

3402 Wisdom: intelligence; higher education/knowledge; teacher/student.

3468 Urgenta: urgency, immediate action; important; dire situation.

318794 Uglia: ugly; unpleasant.

7707 Yes: use to cast a chart, like Horary, asking a "yes" or "no" question. Look for nodal activations, and contact with chart the chart ruler, when looking for general self-direction.

Food Related
2940 Bacon
3061 Cook
3015 Candy
6271 Farmer
10985 Feast
38070 Red Wine
1079 Mimosa
7377 Pizzarello
14917 Taco
7232 Porco: pig.
88705 Potato
133243 Essen: to eat.
15150 Salsa: to eat or dance.

Numerology and Synchronicity:

11111 Repunit: a repunit ("repeated unity") is a number consisting solely of number one. Infinite.

Keywords: numerology; the symbolism of the number one: initiator, beginning of a new cycle. Most would then follow up with "independent" and that's where I may disagree, simply because the key here is repetition and there are technically five number ones in this asteroid number, so that loses its "independence". In tarot, the one card is the Magician, and there are some tricks/illusions at play here as well. Is there really an end or is everything a repeated beginning? This may be a place where a person gets stuck in a repetitive cycle aka "repunit". Or maybe the key to breaking the cycle is accepting "oneness". Singularity.

111111: the number one, six times. Synchronicity. Angel number for self- trust and independence. Message to you from the spiritual realm to focus on your wishes and intentions needed for self-manifesting.

6666 Fro: old dialect for the word "from". Some have connected this to the Norse goddess Freyr. In numerology, four sixes adds up to twenty-four, which reduces down to the number six. It is connected to balance, love, and beauty. Harmony in relationships.

55555 DNA: genetic and soul DNA; connected to the "source".

Asteroid DNA has five number fives, symbolic of the five-pointed star, pentagram. Like the pattern Venus makes, also known as the pentagram of Venus.

Keywords: ancestry, the paradigm of the soul's journey into the physical body. Ascension of mind, body and soul. The codes to psychic awareness and soul purpose. It could also represent the bond to a person's family and what is being passed down generationally.

115301 Linear: straight line. If it is prominent with a personal planet or the Nodes, life may take many twists and turns. While others may walk a completely strait/direct path their whole lives without ever looking up, down, or around them, indirectly missing important signs. Robotic.

1050 Meta: "beyond" or "after". In the modern world, we see the social media side of "Meta" as Facebook with its infinity symbolism to imply "infinite horizons in the metaverse". The irony that "Facebook" probably won't be here "infinitely" is quite literally "beyond" the mindset of today's society. However, the data and information gathered from the social experiment will have leave an infinite impression on future societies.

Meta is also the name of an extremely powerful archangel named Metatron. Some references claim he is Enoch after his body ascended into the heavens. He is said to hold the Book of Life, which records the actions of all beings (Akashic Records). The angel of the veil.

Metatron's Cube in sacred geometry contains all five Platonic solids hidden inside, symbolizing the underlying patterns of our universe. A reminder of what we are capable of while healing the body, mind, and soul.

4003 Schumann: Schumann resonance is a series of electromagnetic waves that occur between the Earth's surface and the ionosphere. Often referred to as the Earth's heartbeat. Its effects on humans, is well known within the enlightened/spiritual communities. Frequencies affect mood, emotions, inner-peace, sleep quality, meditation enhancement, and cognitive improvements. If this asteroid is in aspect to Neptune, Jupiter, or Mercury the person may be highly attuned to the frequencies within their communities and more sensitive to certain sounds and imagery.

999999: there are six number nines represented in this asteroid. In numerology, it adds up to fifty-four, which then reduces to nine. Nine is considered the highest number representing completion/ascension. Indicative of learning and growth. For those with life path number nine, they are here to show humanity compassion and help others grow into their own paths. Honest, truth seekers.

333333: there are six number threes in this name. It's a powerful number that contains the "holy trinity" of number synchronization using the base three, six, nine combination. 333333 adds up to eighteen, which breaks down to nine. Nikola Tesla believed the numbers three, six, and nine held the key to the universe. It's a powerful connection to higher spiritual realms. In the chart, it may indicate a place where someone receives important divine messages to pay close attention to the sign/house this asteroid falls in. For example, is the asteroid in the person's natal third house? The reader should take a closer look at this area in the person's chart. Especially if the natal Jupiter is in third house or aspecting any personal planets or karmic points in the third, sixth, or ninth houses. It could help the individual connect with their personal spirit guide for clarity in matters. They may hold powerful manifestation abilities through creative pursuits.

Personal example: this asteroid is in my natal sixth house conjunct my Vertex (heavy karmic point). It is conjunct my natal Tyche (goddess of luck) and trines my natal Venus.

121212: synchronized number sequence that carries its own frequency. The sequence has three number twelves. 121212 breaks down to nine. Here, we see the numbers three, six, and nine incorporated into the pattern. This sequence is attributed to Divine ascension. A peak in spiritual energy. It assists the soul to initiate breaking free from karmic cycles.

A personal example: this asteroid is in my ninth house in a one-degree orb conjunction with my natal Neptune, Moon, and South Node. I do a lot of spiritual manifesting work with the Moon and Neptune, having this asteroid here helps me give and receive messages that may need to be delivered.

131313: synchronized number sequence that reduces to three. This pattern shows where cycles of choosing oneself over a co-dependent situation. It depicts opening and closing self-imposed cycles that no longer serve the soul. If this asteroid is in the first house, the native may be here to break a cycle of being used or stuck in situations that no longer bring joy. If harshly aspected the person may not feel that they will attain personal fulfillment. If it is the natal third house, the individual will be more willing to choose joy and the pursuit of happiness.

292929: heavy karmic point in the chart, especially if this lands on the 29th degree of a sign, special attention should be put into making sure lessons don't keep getting repeated. Karma breaking point.

9669 Symmetria: symmetric symbols; name suggested by the palindromic shape of the numeral 9669, and the fact that each pair of its digits is invariant under a rotation of 180 degrees. Possibly prominent in charts for those who follow patterns, numerology, and practice gematria.

11302 Rubicon: point of no return. A bounding or limiting line, especially if the line is crossed, the person will not have a favorable outcome. It should be used as a boundary enforcer, not letting people take advantage to the extent an extreme outcome could come out of such a situation. If a person is involved with witchcraft, a binding spell could be used to set limits and use protection magic by knowing where transit Rubicon is located.

11119 Taro(t): tarot cards; using symbolic imagery with numerology. May indicate gifted tarot card readers; metaphysical pursuits; spiritual beliefs.

337380 Lenormand: famous French fortune teller known for tarot cards.

24680 AllEven: all even numbers.

Keywords: balanced. Even. Could it help balance a chart by opposing a heavy stellium? It could be possible for it to offer "balance" in transits as well. Sacred geometry.

Note: magic squares are generally classified according to their order as "odd" if "n", evenly even aka "doubly even" if "n" is a multiple of four, oddly even.

13579 Allodd: the number of this minor planet consists of all odd digits, in increasing order. "All odd."

Keywords: having to do with numbers. Out of balance. Being "odd". Maybe something "uneven". Some believe odd numbers are luckier than even numbers from a superstitious standpoint. A general interest in numerology. Sacred geometry.

4321 Zero: nothingness. Void; empty. Beginning. Hollow. Null. The number of this asteroid is in the form of a countdown.

444 Gyptis: number four in numerology relates to roots, foundation, physical body energy, hard work, and completeness. There are four seasons, four main elements, four directions (north, south, east and west). Number four also has the energy of crossroads and tests that a human soul in a body must go through to reach enlightenment.

Note: Additional meaning for this asteroid found in the Health list.

Indigenous:

9480 Inti: the Sun god in Inca religion, also called Apu-Punchau, believed to be the ancestor of the Incas. Inti was at the head of the state cult. He was usually represented in human form, his face portrayed as a gold disk from which rays and flames extended. Inti's sister was the Moon, Mama-Kilya, who was portrayed as a silver disk with human features.

9484 Wanambi: the Australian Aborigines' best-known spirit, the Rainbow Snake, which is the rainbow and the revealer of truth. Often seen as a creator god; named for the obvious identification between the shape of a rainbow and the shape of a snake. Some scholars believe that the link between snake and rainbow suggests the cycle of the seasons and the importance of water in human life. When the rainbow is seen in the sky, it is said to be the Rainbow Serpent moving from one waterhole to another, and the divine concept explained why some water holes never dried up when drought struck. There are innumerable names and stories associated with the serpent, all of which communicate the significance and power of this being within Aboriginal traditions. It is viewed as a giver of life, through its association with water, but can be a destructive force if angry.

9489 Tanemahuta: god of forests and birds; designed woman by molding her from the soil (earth).

7480 Norwan: goddess of light of the Wintun (Wintu) Native American peoples of Northern California. Norwan relates to daylight, for she dances all day, never stops while there is light. Her title of Bastepomas, food-giving, is also significant, and helps show that she is the warm, dancing air which we see close to the Earth in fine weather, which is requisite for plant growth. Norwan, food; the flooding light on the Earth.

Keywords: the translation was hard to come by. She would be like a warm, nurturing Ceres/Demeter (without the cold side). Unless harshly aspected in the chart, however that isn't her primary nature. She would most likely soften a harsh aspect. She's also very hardworking. A provider. Caregiver. It wouldn't surprise me at all to see her strong in a single mother's chart as the primary caregiver, or any sort of caregiver, multitasking (dancing) her way seamlessly through life in the eyes of her children. This is a strong woman. Capable. Burnt out (light) tired when all the days chores are finally done. Unceasing power to rise again like the

Sun to do it all over again another day.

4105 Tsia: Zia Sun symbol used by the Zia people in New Mexico. Their symbol, a red circle with groups of rays pointing in four directions. Four is the sacred number of the Zia and can be found repeated in the four points radiating from the circle. The number four is embodied in:
- the four points of the compass (north, south, east and west);
- the four seasons of the year (spring, summer, autumn and winter);
- the four periods of each day (morning, noon, evening and night);
- the four seasons of life (childhood, youth, middle years and old age)
- the four sacred obligations one must develop (a strong body, a clear mind, a pure spirit, and devotion to the welfare of others).

Keywords: sacred knowledge passed through generations; number four life path in numerology, compass to the four corners of the soul/chart. Tsia would be karmically important if conjunct the Nodes or a person's Vertex.

Vedic:

4486 Mithra: Iranian version of Vedic Mitra; guardian of human order; represents friendship, integrity, harmony, honesty, and meetings.

20000 Varuna: guardian of cosmic order; god of water, justice, truth.

2415 Ganesa: Vedic god of astrology. Removes obstacles. God of happiness and children. Guidance and inspiration when using the science of light (astrology). High intellect. Unwavering devotion. Represents the benefic planet Jupiter.

4034 Vishnu: preserver and protector of the universe.

5863 Tara: great wisdom and manifestation goddess. Protection and healing.

817 Annika: Anika is another name of the Hindu goddess Durga. She is the warrior goddess, whose mythology centers around combating evils and demonic forces that threaten peace, prosperity, and dharma (karma) of the good. She is the fierce form of the protective mother goddess, willing to unleash her anger against wrong, violence for liberation and destruction to empower creation.

Goddess of victory; victory of good over evil; the Invincible One. Durga is depicted in the Hindu pantheon as a goddess riding a lion or tiger, with many arms each carrying a weapon. Wife of Shiva and another form of Parvati. She is celebrated as a Supreme Being and the creator of the universe.

2847 Parvati: goddess of fertility, love and devotion; as well as of divine strength and power.

4227 Kaali: goddess of death, time, and doomsday and is often associated with sexuality and violence but is also considered a strong mother-figure and symbolic of motherly-love. Kali also embodies shakti; feminine energy, creativity and fertility, and is an incarnation of Parvati.

1170 Siva: (Shiva) destroyer god of the universe in order to re-create it. Hindus believe his powers of destruction and recreation are used even now to destroy the illusions and imperfections of this world, paving the way for beneficial change.

22817 Shankar: another version of Shiva; "one who brings about happiness or prosperity".

10819 Mahakala: another version of Shiva; god of time, maya, creation, destruction and power.

4401 Aditi: unbound sky goddess; , honored as the mother creator of life because she gave birth to the planets and the stars; the guardian of all life and the supporter of all creatures. She is also the keeper of light that illuminates all life and ensures consciousness.

9172 Abhramu: a sky/cloud goddess that was magical but got cursed by a sage and became an elephant.

5881 Akashi: Akashic Records of the heaven/sky; indestructible tablets of the astral light.

2629 Rudra: supreme lord; "roarer"; associated with wind, storms and hunt. Terror; most frightening; another version of Shiva.

3811 Karma: the sum of a person's actions in this and previous states of existence, viewed as deciding their fate in future existences. ***Note***: *good to use when checking transits.*

22533 Krishnan: (Krishna) most popular of the Hindu gods, is revered as a supreme deity and the eighth incarnation of the god Vishnu. Worshiped as a restorer of order to the world; prophecy foretelling of what is to come; something that is predicted.

5239 Reiki: healing technique based on the principle that the therapist can channel energy into the patient by means of touch, to activate the natural healing processes of the patient's body and restore physical and emotional well-being.

Personal note: If a person has this asteroid exactly conjunct natal Pluto and is a Human Design Reflector (one who has no chakra definition), reiki could do potential harm to this person if they are not in awareness that the energy the practitioner is using just reflects the practitioner themselves, not the Reflector aura which repels and is "Teflon".

12472 Samadhi: enlightenment, nirvana, spiritual ecstasy; self- mastery.

1779 Prana: life force, yogic breathing.

20851 Ramachandran: prince married to Sita; embodiment of true love ***Note***: *use in synastry charts along with Sita 244.*

244 Sita: wife of Rama; They were a model loyal and loving couple.

2307 Garuda: a bird, mount of Vishnu, related to kundalini awakening.

2211 Hanuman: Hindu deity; protector from harm.

23681 Prabhu: means master or the prince in Sanskrit and many of the Indian languages; it is a name sometimes applied to God. Royalty.

23323 Anand: pleasure or joy; spiritual bliss.

4106 Nada: divine music, sound heard when kundalini activated.

2825 Soma: drink/elixir that invokes bliss, immortality.

25290 Vibhuti: sacred ash; valuable.

8100 Nobeyama: Nobe (noble) Yama (Hindu god of death) final judge of souls.

2415 Ganesa: remover of obstacles.

3321 Dasha: in Vedic astrology means "condition", "state", "circumstance", "period of life", or "planetary period". It is considered very important in Vedic astrology, therefore, tracking its transits could prove beneficial.

243 Ida: in Hindu mythology Ida is the goddess of speech and knowledge.

Egyptian:

4257 Ubasti: cat goddess Bast, Bastet, Moon and Sun goddess of love and children; goddess of Divine protection, pleasure, good health and most associated with cats. Bastet is said to be the gentler version of Sekhmet her warrior counterpart. Bastet protected Ra from his enemies.

42 Isis: mother, queen, Moon, magic goddess; Isis wants to make things whole again. She picks up the pieces, and she can represent completion.

1923 Osiris: god of the dead, afterlife, underworld, rebirth and god of the Moon. He is the symbol of resurrection. New beginnings, spiritually shedding who we were told to be, and walking towards our correct path.

56551 Seth (Set): Seth killed Osiris to take the throne of Egypt but was defeated by Horus. Set was known as chaos and destruction. Violence and warfare. He is associated with earthquakes, thunderstorms and eclipses. In the natal chart, a person should pay attention to where this asteroid is transitioning in a violent event chart.

3554 Amun: Amon Ra, Sun creator god. Some believe the "Lord's Prayer" recited by Christianity is a prayer for Amun. Just like saying "Amen" after a prayer. Most known as the Sun god.

1924 Horus: The Sun god depicted with a falcon head, and one eye. In a natal chart he can manifest many ways. Depending on placements, he could show where a person may have had a difficult childhood and is here to break a generational trauma cycle. One part of his story, that is often overlooked, is his ability to reconcile opposites. Not merge them together but bring them all to his table peacefully as "third" eye. Combining them and creating a whole new entity from the other two elements.

257 Nephthys: guardian of the dead, who also had healing and protection magic. She is associated with hawks and kites. In modern times, she may portray a time of mourning or grief. She carries the element of air.

1912 Anubis: is all about weighing up our actions and deeds, considering the consequences of our behavior on others and taking responsibility for our actions. He can represent a literal death or transformations. He weighs the heart of the soul before deciding its resting place. In the chart, look for a connection to Venus, or the fifth house. How pure is your heart? Have you checked in on your heart chakra lately? Is your heart heavy and weighed down? What actions can you take to lighten the load for someone else?

5351 Sekhmet: goddess of war, wrath, magic with a lioness head, called also Mighty One. She was the image of courage and resilience. Her first instinct is usually one of destruction, however, she chooses carefully who and how to use her healing powers. Strategic.

2100 Ra-Shalom: Ra (the Sun God); patron of heaven, creation, power and light. In a chart, if Ra is conjunct a person's natal Sun, they may "shine brighter" or stand out in the crowd. A magnetic aura of attraction. However, if this asteroid is in harsh aspect with the Moon, the person may not feel "seen" as if they are being eclipsed by the Sun. They may have low self-esteem or feel unworthy of affection if asteroid Ra squares the natal Venus or Chiron.

1513 Imhotep: great architect and counselor "The one who comes in peace". He wrote and maintained ancient/sacred texts that included advanced healing techniques. His connection with healing has often been associated with the Greek equivalent Asklepios.

4848 Tutankhamun: famous young pharaoh "King Tut".

216 Kleopatra: Cleopatra, Queen of Egypt; she represents beauty and lust. Extremely intelligent, she spent many hours in a lab using alchemy for healing tonics, or beauty enhancement. She is known to speak possibly up to nine languages, making her an asset to diplomatic relations.

3199 Nefertiti: great Egyptian queen; mother of King Tut.

15456 Caesar: Julius Caesar, Roman leader and warrior who loved Queen Cleopatra. Sometimes used in synastry to find partners who empower their partners with knowledge and wisdom.

5249 Giza: ancient location of the great pyramids.

17936 Nilus: the Nile River, and the name of a Greek/Roman god embodying the river.

Sirius: Alpha Canis Minor: basis of Egyptian life. Heliac Sirio Rising marked the beginning of Egyptian year and flooding Nile season. Alnitak, Alnilam, Mintaka: the three Stars of Orion Belt, aligned with the Pyramids of Giza.

Religious, Faith, and Saints:

192158 Christian: Christianity.
3241 Yeshuhua (Jesus): "to rescue", "to deliver", "to save".
965 Angelica: angel.
223 Rosa: Saint Rose of Lima; healer, roses, cared for the needy.
208 Lacrimosa: tearful, sorrows, from the Catholic Church mass prayer: Full of tears will be that day when from the ashes shall arise.
Keywords: sorrow, tearful, tragedy, mournful, empathy, emotional.
9395 Saintmichael: Archangel Michael; guardian, protector, champion of justice, healer of the sick. Divine intervention.
Associated with fixed star Aldebaran, "watcher of the east" located at 9 Gemini in the Taurus constellation (one of the four royal stars).
1200 Imperatrix: empress; "to order, to command". Ruling female. Goddess ruling the world. Royalty. It was also used to address the Virgin Mary. "Ruler of the Angels".
85195 Von Helfta: Gertrud von Helfta. German mystic; Gertrude the Great; Saint Gertrude; the age of twenty-five, she experienced the first of a series of visions that continued throughout her life. She showed tender sympathy for souls in Purgatory. In modern times, it would represent the souls in mental illness, addiction, lost and hopeless. She is where one finds empathy no matter what their situation and helps them see the light.
1237 Genevieve: saint, falsely accused, sentenced to death, avenged by the executioner. One taking the blame for something that they didn't do.
3276: Porta Coeli: Heaven's Gate; portal; Bridge to Heaven.
11911 Angel: angel; Divine intervention. (Good to look for the transits for people who may be experiencing difficulties, the angel transit can show up and help them find the light.)
296577 Arkhangelsk: archangel of justice, guardian of the church, and known healer. Warrior for the children. Patronage saint of sick, suffering dying people, poor souls, bankers, grocers, and military. Chivalry. Associated with mountains and safe passages for mariners.
798 Ruth: spiritual qualities, such as compassion, unfailing devotion, respect, grace, honesty, integrity, generosity, wholesomeness, virtue, honor, and kindness.
10343 Church

321485 Cross

28795 Bibles

15417 Babylon: is the symbol of the "anti-Christ" system in modern day Christianity.

355 Gabriella: Archangel Gabriel; prophecy and translator; "God is my strength"; mediator; receiving good news; encouragement and clarity. Gabriel rules the root chakra; color frequency- white; he is also known as Fomalhault, one of the four royal fixed stars. Fomalhault is located at 3 Pisces. Ability to speak and communicate clearly.

1930 Lucifer: fallen angel of light; meanings for him are extremely interchangeable depending on placement and transit.

Note: I have found interesting synastry connections using asteroid Lilith #1181 with Lucifer. If a person has a prominent Venus in their chart, sometimes I will check where asteroid Lucifer is because of the symbolism with the "morning star". It is especially noteworthy, if the person has a morning star Venus in strong aspect with asteroid Lucifer. The Venus may "shine" brighter for this person, and have a very Venusian aesthetic.

318 Magdalena: witnessed the burial and resurrection of Jesus Christ. She is a saint in the Catholic religion. "Apostle of the Apostles."

708 Raphaela: Archangel Raphael; heavenly messenger, healer and protector. Patron of the blind, nurses, doctors, travelers, and happy meetings. *See fixed star Regulus at 29 Leo.*

92891 Bless: receiving and giving blessings.

26333 Joachim: means "raised by Yahweh". Saint Joachim was the father of Mary (Jesus' mother). Connected to lambs and doves.

19119 Dimpna: Saint Dymphna. She was hunted down and beheaded. Murdered by her father after she ran away when she heard her father had intentions of bedding her and making her his wife. Attributes: crown, sword, lily, and lamp. She was the patron saint of mental disorders, neurological disorders, runaways, victims of incest, depression, anxiety.

234 Barbara: Saint Barbara, patron saint of artillerymen. She is also traditionally the patron saint of armorers, military engineers, gunsmiths, tunnellers, miners and anyone else who worked with weaponry and explosives. She is invoked against thunder and lightning and all accidents arising from explosions of gunpowder. She is venerated by Catholics who face the danger of sudden and violent death in work.

22540 Mork: aka Magog. Part of the end of days prophecy as the leaders of the enemy nations against God's people. Gog and Magog are said to engage in human cannibalism in the romances and derived literature. Sons of Satan.

Note: *Mork Is also a Slang term for aliens in the British science fiction television series The Aliens (TV series).*

Keywords: enemy, invasion, war, revelation, revolution, uprising, chaos, aliens, evil, foreign; fear of the unknown; social reform; protesting; historical wars.

3551 Verenia: one of the two first Vestal virgins consecrated by the legendary Roman king, Numa Pompilius.

Keywords: celibacy, devoting oneself to higher spirituality and beliefs. Look for aspects to natal Vesta.

576 Emanuela: "God will protect us" in the Bible. Saint Emmanuel is the patron saint of garlic, soap makers, and "ladies of the night". Also called "The Comforter".

741 Botolphia: Boltoph of Thorney. The patron saint of boundaries, trade, and travel. Various aspects of farming. Feast day is June 17th or 25th depending on location.

1288 Santa: saintly, holy, and blessed.

441 Bathilde: saint of "elite birth" and later a queen. She was beautiful, intelligent, modest, and attentive to the needs of others. Even as queen, Balthilde remained humble and modest. She is famous for her charitable service and generous donations. As queen, she was a capable states woman. She abolished the practice of trading Christian slaves and strove to free children who had been sold into slavery. She was a huge advocate for enslaved children, because she herself was sold as a child slave in her own youth.

Keywords: this asteroid may show up in someone with a "Cinderella" story. As well as someone who actively fights for children who are victimized by adults. The one who protects the underdog. This is a modest person who does not like the spotlight but can climb the social ladder and never forget those left behind or helped her to get there. Social work. Child advocate specialist. Generous, kindhearted. Empathetic. Fights social injustice. Freedom.

583 Klotilde: Saint Clotilde; known for her kind and giving nature, almsgiving, and mercy. Triumph in battle; the patron saint of queens, widows, brides, and those in exile. She was the patroness of the lame, those who came to a violent death, and women who suffered from ill-tempered husbands. She is connected to a spring fountain that is believed to cure skin diseases in Les Andelys, France.

586 Thekla: Saint Thecla; known for many escapes from near death experiences. Well known role-model for women.

Keywords: survivor, mentor, miraculous event, escape danger, lucky, divine intervention; miracles.

357 Ninina: Saint Ninian is acknowledged as Scotland's first saint, however, his story is very private and hidden. Mostly he had the power to cure illness and perform miracles. Due to the secretive nature, its possible he represents a hidden talent.

999 Zachia: means "pure" or "intelligent". Innocent. From the Bible: "Blessed are the pure of heart, for they shall see God."

205 Martha: from the Bible. Martha is said to have witnessed the birth of Jesus. She is known as Saint Martha in the Catholic church. Name could translate to "mistress", "the lady", or "master". Through time, the cult of Martha developed, the images of maturity, strength, common sense, and corn for others. The "noble hostess" with the reputation for overseeing housework and chores.

282 Clorinde: character from "Jerusalem Delivered", a poem by the Italian poet Torquato Tasso. Warrior woman; she saves Christians from enemy attacks. She is accidently killed by her lover during a night battle, he didn't recognize her in armor. She converted to Christianity before dying.

Clorinde is also a species of white butterflies. Using the symbolism of a butterfly's transformation by embracing spirituality in death, emphasizes the cycle of rebirth. The place we fight our internal spiritual battles and become reborn, transformed/enlightened. Look for connections to asteroid Psyche #16.

298 Baptistina: Baptist; baptized. Cleansing sins. Purity. Rebirth.

416 Vaticana: the Catholic Church Vatican.

6710 Apostel: apostle; a person who preaches the gospel; disciple.

4390 Madreteresa: Mother Teresa; Catholic saint.

7366 Agata: also spelled Agatha; her name means "good". Saint Agatha of Sicily; she is the patron saint of breast cancer patients, eruptions of Mount Etna. *Note*: *interesting to find this one next to Chiron for cancer patients and recovery.*

752 Sulamitis: Biblical woman identified with the queen of Sheba. Mysterious woman who went to test King Solomon's wisdom herself. Once he proved himself, she lavished him with gifts and spices. He returned the favor and lavished her as well. The story is much debated among religious scholars. Possibly affiliated with the "Song of Solomon".

Keywords: mysterious. A place where one must "see it for themselves". It could also portend wealth, high social status, respect, wisdom, faith and truth. Possible long distance love affairs. Peace.

The Royal Fixed Stars
Regulus: Archangel Raphael at 29 Leo.
Aldebaren: Archangel Michael at 9 Gemini.
Antares: Archangel Uriel at 9 Sagittarius.
Formalhaut: Archangel Gabriel at 3 Pisces.

Artistic, Creative, and Philosophical:

33 Polyhymnia: muse of sacred music. Prophetic hymns and poetry. Shows strongly in musician and artists charts. Musical contributions. Connection to harmonics.

She is connected to the Oracles of Dodoma. The auspicious number thirty-three. She is also the muse of geometry and meditation. The ability to reach other dimensions and bring back her knowledge by sharing it through writing, song arts, and expressionism.

22 Kalliope: she is the muse of poetry and writing. Such a beautiful place for her if she is conjunct Venus or Mercury. Musical and writing talents.

80 Sappho: muse of poetry and writing. Mostly open-minded inspiration. She was known for her bisexual orientation and many poets wrote about her in their poetry. She had many talents, therefore she is on several lists for her interchangeable meanings.

23 Thalia: muse of comedy; the joyous or flourishing one; happiness.

Keywords: comedian; bringer of joy; blessing; humor; charismatic.

3367 Orpheus: famous singer, the son of Calliope, whose songs were so beautiful that he could charm every living being, down to the stones in the earth. He was taught by the god of music, Apollo. He is often used in synastry charts alongside asteroid Eurydice, his lost love, whom he would go into the underworld to try and get Hades to release. If this asteroid is prominent in a musician's chart, they most likely use their own personal tragedies and transform them into incredible/memorable works of art.

1266 Tone: musical or vocal sound with reference to pitch, quality, and strength. Alternatively, the general character, feel, or attitude of a place, piece of writing, or situation. Choice of words. Language attitude. Sound. Mood. Spirit. Temper or feeling.

3451 Mentor: someone who imparts wisdom to and shares knowledge with a less experienced colleague. Wise teacher. Encouraging.

12238 Actor: to perform, to play a role, to pretend; theatrical, fame, to put on dramatic productions, performance art.

1163 Saga: goddess of tales and myths. She would drink heavily from her walls and transcribe the important events of the day so that none would be forgotten. She is the patroness of seers and writers, and she records the history of the world as well as events to come.

Keywords: prophecy; writer; blogger; historian; foresight; journalism; storyteller.

104 Klymene: The goddess of fame, renown, and infamy.

Keywords: famous; well- known; fame; accomplished; high achievements.

Shadow side: stage fright; low achievers; not gaining recognition.

195 Eurykleia: Greek nurse (nanny) of Odysseus. Name means "broad fame". Eurycleia is the only person to recognize Odysseus without him first revealing himself after he returns home from the Trojan War. After he enters his own house as a guest disguised as a beggar, Eurycleia bathes him and recognizes him by a scar. She is also known as a snitch, pointing out other servants who have been dishonest in his absence. (They got hung because she told on them.)

Keywords: become famous. Uncaring of others who stood with you before fame and fortune; devoted caregiver, nanny, may show up in charts of people who are raised by nannies who care for children of the wealthy class, somewhat raising them as their own. Devoted and faithful to a very select few. One who knows all about the household's dirty secrets behind the scenes. Modern day celebrity gossip.

26950 Legendre: legend.

Keywords: notorious; well-known; legacy; fame; accomplished and recognized.

2989 Imago: means "image". Self-image or projected image. How you view yourself or others. Photograph. Viewpoint/perspective. What others see. Ego. Viewers and followers.

4572 Brage: god of writing and poetic arts, music and creativity.

657 Gunlod: in Norse mythology, she was the daughter of a giant. She guarded the gate of poetry or art.

Keywords: in astrology, she is said to be where hidden talents are to be discovered or "unlocked". What is your hidden potential? Track planetary transits, when Gonlod is being activated in your chart, what is Gunlod calling you to try?

2063 Bacchus: Roman god of wine and revelry (Dionysus). Excessive pleasure seeking; overindulgence; if conjunct Neptune, may show addictions, self-destruction, or refusing to live in reality. Needs grounding.

22725 Drabble: is a short work of fiction of one hundred words in length. The purpose of the drabble is brevity, testing the author's ability to express interesting and meaningful ideas in a confined space.

Note: *Modern day "X" or Twitter that had character limits for post.*

Keywords: writing, poetry, being artistically confined, or practice learning boundaries. Limited space for expression; artistic blockage; Haiku poets.

57 Mnemosyne: means "memory". She was the Titaness daughter of Gaia and Uranus and is the mother of the Nine Muses by Zeus. It was said that kings and poets received their talents via Mnemosyne and her daughters. My favorite tale is about her presiding over a pool in Hades, where souls were encouraged to drink from her depths to forget their past before their next reincarnation.

Keywords: memory, memories, dreams of the past, past people returning, deep, hidden talents, sudden knowing without understanding why, past life memories and experiences. Drinking the Kool-Aid. Escapism.

4769 Castalia: Greek nymph who Apollo turned into a fountain at Delphi. Castalia could inspire the genius of poetry, writing, and arts to those who drank from her waters or listened to their quiet sounds. The sacred water was also used to clean the Delphi temples. Connected to receiving highly gifted, spiritual/Divine intelligence through the water. It's possible the water could have been "altered" to create hallucinations to achieve higher spiritual consciousness.

She should be studied in charts for writers, artists, and philosophers. Possibly people who use substances to achieve enlightenment.

8052 Novalis: Novalis' personal world view, informed by his education, philosophy, professional knowledge, and pietistic background, has become known as "magical idealism"; a name derived from Novalis' reference in his 1798 notebooks to a type of literary prophet, the Magischer Idealist (magical idealist). In this world view, philosophy and poetry are united. Magical idealism is Novalis' synthesis of the German idealism of Fichte and Schelling with the creative imagination. The goal of a creative imagination is to break down the barriers between language and world, as well as the subject and object. The magic is the enlivening of nature as it responds to our will.

96189 Pygmalion: god of Ancient Greek mythology and name of the Greek sculptor who fell in love with his statue, Galatea, which then came to life. The "Pygmalion effect" is the phenomenon whereby higher expectations lead to an increase in performance, forms of self-fulfilling prophecy. By the Pygmalion effect, people internalize their positive labels, and those with positive labels succeed accordingly. The idea behind the Pygmalion effect is that increasing the leader's expectation of the follower's performance will result in better follower performance. High expectations lead to improved performance, and as such, low expectations lead to poor performance. Perception and expectation may possibly be found in a similar part in the brain.

Keywords: having high expectations; setting what seems to be unattainable goals. Believing in something so much, you breathe it into existence. Mind over matter. Is the glass half full or half empty? Single-minded focus. Meditation into manifestation. Setting the tone.

6312 RobHeinlein: American science fiction author best known for his works "The Moon is a Harsh Mistress" and "Starship Troopers".

Heinlein repeatedly addressed certain social themes: the importance of individual liberty and self-reliance, the obligation individuals owe to their societies, the influence of organized religion on culture and government, and the tendency of society to repress nonconformist thoughts. He also speculated on the influence of space travel on human cultural practices.

Keywords: non-conformist, being creative by finding a voice in a close-minded society, understanding that you won't be around to see your futuristic vision be relevant. Grasping the idea of futurism. Speaking out against corruption/propaganda. Calling out the followers that are unable to see the big picture. Gifted visionary. Social reformer. Activist. Free speech.

9922 Catcheller: U.S. writer Joseph Heller (1923–1999) endowed the English language with a new term in the 1961 novel, Catch-22, by epitomizing both the problems of a sane person in an insane society and the absurdity of war. "Damned if you do, damned if you don't." "Catch hell."

6614 Antisthenes: philosopher; founder of the Cynic school of philosophy. He was a pupil of Socrates. He taught people can gain happiness by rigorous training and by living in a way which is natural for themselves, rejecting all conventional desires for wealth, power, sex, and fame. Instead, they were to lead a simple life free from all possessions. He preferred pain over pleasure. An underground cult began and the Cynics adopted Hercules as their hero, epitomizing the ideal Cynic. Heracles brought Cerebus, the hound of Hades, from the underworld, a point of special appeal to the dogman. The ideal Cynic would evangelize; as the watchdog of humanity, they thought it their duty to hound people about the error of their ways. The example of the Cynic's life (and the use of the Cynic's biting satire) would dig up and expose the pretensions which lay at the root of everyday conventions.

Keywords: cynical, critical, rude, watchful, withdrawn, opinionated, judgmental of society. Connection with dogs. Watch dog. Vigilante justice. No pain, no gain. Minimalist. Exposing deep, hidden secrets and truth. Rejecting materialism and social "trends". Cultlike "off the grid" lifestyle.

14526 Xenocrates: Greek philosopher; distinguished three forms of being: sense, intellect, and opinion. He considered unity and duality to be gods which rule the universe, and the soul a self-moving number. He believed in mediating between knowledge and sensuous perception. All three modes of apprehension partake of truth. He connected the above three stages of knowledge with the three Fates: Atropos, Clotho, and Lachesis.

3360 Syrinx: a nymph known for her chastity. She was being perused by the god Pan and asked her sisters for help to escape his obsession with her. (Guarding her virtue.) She was transformed into hollow water reeds that made a haunting sound when the god's frustrated breath blew across them. Pan cut the reeds to fashion the first set of "Pan pipes" which were thenceforth known as syrinx.

Keywords: musical instrument talents, haunting music. Connected to the larynx or vocal box. Trance inducting music.

Other possible connection:

In the medical world, a syrinx is a fluid filled cavity in the spinal cord or brain stem. Predisposing factors include craniocervical junction abnormalities, previous spinal cord trauma, and spinal cord tumors. Symptoms include flaccid weakness of the hands and arms and deficits in pain and temperature sensation in a cape like distribution over the back and neck. Light touch, position, and vibration sensation are not affected.

11965 Catullus: 1st century Roman poet. The explicit sexual imagery which he uses in some of his poems has shocked many readers; the erotic poems are about his homosexual desires and acts, but most are about women. Some of his poems were very crude, vulgar and obscene. He greatly admired Sappho and was the source of what we know about her.

Keywords: writer, poet; homosexuality; bisexual; erotica; crude; pornography; sexual desires; if harshly aspected, possibly a hard time expressing one's fetishes in a healthy manner or feeling shame for having certain desires.

Shadow side: sexual abuse.

95 Arethusa: sea nymph who fled her home and became a fountain. Water spirit; fresh stream of water; using water to escape danger or capture; healing through water therapy. (Hydrotherapy.)

Keywords: float/water therapy; escapism; extreme emotions; empathy.

11059 Nulliusinverba: "Nullius in Verba", variously translated as "On the words of no one", "Nothing in words", or "Respect the facts". To verify all statements by an appeal to facts determined by experiment. Using logic over emotion.

4348 Poulydamas: the closest counselor and strategist for the Trojan prince, Hector. Poulydamas was given the gift of better judgement by the gods. He tried to advise and warn for the gates of Troy to be closed off to Achilles, but Hector left the city and confronted Achilles anyway. In the natal chart, this could be a place where a person is able to be the voice of reason, have better judgment, and not be emotionally reactive. On the shadow side, in harsh aspect, it could show where a person lacks sound judgement and responds impulsively. Example: if conjunct natal Mars in Aries squaring Neptune blurs the lines of clear minded decision making.

12715 Godin: 18th century French astronomer who proposed to send expeditions to the equator and the polar sea, to measure in both places an arc of one degree to find out the true shape of the Earth.

Isn't it ironic that they name asteroids in space after people who didn't believe in the shape of the earth?

Possible keywords: explorer, conspiracy theorists, issues trusting authority or indoctrinated education systems, one who must "see it to believe it".

11298 Gide: French author. His work can be seen as an investigation of freedom and empowerment in the face of moralistic and puritanical constraints, and centers on his continuous effort to achieve intellectual honesty. His self-exploratory texts reflect his search for how to be fully oneself, including owning one's sexual nature, without at the same time betraying one's values.

Keywords: extremely relevant considering the current situation of the world. How to express oneself without having to go overboard. Pure honesty and ethics. He truly grasped how to balance being who you are in a world that may not accept you. How to love yourself and respect yourself without losing your identity in the process of discovery. He understood rebellion requires balance and restraint. Reminds me of a harmonious version of Saturn and Uranus.

Side note: his name "Gide" sounds like "guide" so this could also show up as a literal guide in your chart; where and how you view morals.

11363 Vives: Juan Luis Vives, renaissance humanist. His beliefs on the soul, insight into early medical practice, and perspective on emotions, memory, and learning earned him the title of the "father" of modern psychology. He is considered the first scholar to analyze the psyche directly. Vives expressed an interest in the soul. He believed that understanding how the soul functions is more valuable than understanding the soul itself. "He was not concerned with what the soul is, but rather what the soul was like". He believed that the best part of the soul is its ability to understand, remember, reason, and judge; How we perceive a painted picture is more telling than declaring what the picture is itself. He was also a strong advocate for those with mental illness. He paved the way for getting the mentally ill real help instead of mocking them and doing more damage.

Keywords: psychology, philosopher, to understand "why", mental illness advocate; believing in the power to choose; separating logic from emotion; mind over matter.

3116 Goodricke: John Goodricke, 18th century Dutch English deaf-mute astronomer, who is best known for his observations of fixed star Algol. He is credited with discovering it as an eclipsing binary star. Algol is one of the most famous fixed stars, thus following the transit of Goodricke is important for people with strong Algol charts.

11020 Orwell: George Orwell is the author of Animal Farm and Nineteen Eighty-Four. His writings are well known as "Orwellian", an adjective describing a situation, idea, or societal condition that George Orwell identified as being destructive to the welfare of a free and open society. It denotes an attitude and a brutal policy of draconian control by propaganda, surveillance, misinformation, denial of truth(doublethink), and manipulation of the past; including the "unperson"—a person whose past existence is expunged from the public record and memory, practiced by modern repressive governments.

Keywords: writer/author; a social movement perspective that we are watching take place presently. The people are "waking up", realizing they have been lied to and manipulated by "fake news", media propaganda, or "programming". It is a "question everything" type of awakening. Orwell predicted this or forewarned depending on how you look at it.

Keywords: could represent seeking truth or the opposite extreme of not believing anything or anyone with a tinge of paranoia. It's a place to either break free or remain "controlled". The matrix/rabbit hole, nothing is as it seems, and the truth is stranger than fiction. It could be the free thinker who is scoffed at or called "crazy" for sounding the warning of what the future will be like.

22283 Pytheas: is the first known scientific visitor and reporter of the Arctic, polar ice, and the Germanic tribes. He introduced the idea of distant Thule to geographic imagination, and his account of the tides is the earliest known to suggest the Moon as their cause. His recorded journey has pieces missing. I think that what he discovered was meant to remain a secret.

Keywords: navigation, long journeys, discoveries; sworn secrecy; mysterious anomalies; the unknown; astronomy; Moon and tides.

Navigating a way through secret passageways and depths of personal imagination (that may or may not be imaginary). Wonderland or Neverland.

409 Aspasia: mistress of Pericles; she housed many famous worriers and philosophers including Socrates; some scholars suggest that Aspasia was a brothel keeper and a prostitute.

"To ask questions about Aspasia's life is to ask questions about half of humanity." *Madeleine M. Henry.*

Keywords: she seems to be associated with political writing, teaching/educating and philosophy (intellectualism and politics). I would personally add that she may show up in charts of women involved in political/sexual scandals. However, she is never disgraced, she never loses her reputation among peers even if they try. She is always highly respected for her knowledge and insight; she may show up for people who are master orators and professional speech writers. Journalists. Strong, confident, witty. Well educated; independent.

12576 Oresme: was a significant philosopher of the later Middle Ages. He wrote influential works on economics, mathematics, physics, astrology and astronomy, philosophy, and theology. He was a counselor of King Charles V of France, and probably one of the most original thinkers of 14th century Europe.

What really stands out to me is his work on the divergent series in mathematics. He was able to prove divergent numbers were infinite (do not have a limit). Basically, ruling zero is in fact infinite. Taking this further he was able to prove the harmonic series is the divergent infinite series (harmonic music vibrations, frequencies, and wavelengths).

He had a unique outlook on astrology that I believe is noteworthy.

Oresme argued that it was very probable that the length of the day and the year were incommensurate (irrational), as indeed were the periods of the motions of the Moon and the planets. He noted that planetary conjunctions and oppositions would never recur in exactly the same way. Oresme maintained that this disproves the claims of astrologers who think "they know with punctual exactness the motions, aspects, conjunctions and oppositions... [judge] rashly and erroneously about future events".

(He argues that time does not exist therefore cannot be predicted.)

Some of his beliefs are borderline supportive of the flat earth theory we are seeing so much of these days.

His quote: "Everyone maintains, and I think myself, that the heavens do move and not the Earth."

Side note: Oresme claimed to be an astrologer but rejected the basis of astrology. He is a walking contradiction which is sort of frustrating and intriguing. Because of his work in the math of harmonics, I'm curious if the harmonic charts could be connected to his work. He would be prominent in any person who is considered a "conspiracy theorist".

2135 Aristaeus: god of beekeeping, cheese, and rustic crafts, discovery of many useful arts, most notably, beekeeping. He is the protector of shepherds and their flocks, knowledge of hunting, herbal medicine, and prophecy. (Son of Apollo.)

Keywords: certified in healing arts; do it yourself craft inventions/projects; protection using divination arts; interest in ancient occult knowledge.

Most Popular:

These asteroids are the most used in today's astrology. Because there is an abundance of research and resources available for them, I am keeping this short and simple.

Chiron: wounded healer; the key to unlocking and healing our deepest wound.

1 Ceres (technically a dwarf planet): motherly; nourishing; mother/child relationships; healthy food and agriculture; provider; healthy choices and lifestyle.

Shadow side: over-bearing; critical and insecure; abandonment; control issues; not taking health seriously.

1108 Demeter: same as Ceres above.

2 Pallas: wisdom; knowledge; strategic thinking; healing; and creative outlets; courage; diplomatic; trusting your instincts.

881 Athene: same as Pallas.

3 Juno: often called "the ideal wife", mainly used as a relationship asteroid to see what/where we seek and find committed relationships.

103 Hera: same as Juno.

4 Vesta: protector of the sacred Vestial flame in the home; self-discovery; devotion towards the future of humanity ,"keeper of light".

46 Hestia: same as Vesta.

16 Psyche: her interpretations vary greatly. Her name means "soul" or "butterfly"; the transformation of being reborn, psychology of the soul. Being "purified" by suffering physical or mental issues. The aspects to psyche are most important for interpretation. She is sometimes viewed as empathetic and intuitively aware of others' deep psychological wounds.

Shadow side: cold, apathetic, projecting problems onto others; gaslighting; manipulation.

In synastry: "heart" and "soul" = Eros and Psyche (following the heart).

136199 Eris: (technically a dwarf planet now); throws apples out of the apple cart to stir up mischief and get attention. She has been in Aries since 1926 and will remain there until 2048. Because of this, everyone living in our modern time has natal Eris in Aries. If a person has a natal planet conjunct Eris, she could make that planet's energy more Uranian in nature. It is always good to know when one of our other planets conjuncts her in our chart. For example, when Mars transits into Aries and conjuncts Eris, you may have the sudden urge to break free or have an impulsive, reckless or overly reactive attitude.

Part 2 : Individual Asteroid Deep Dives and Case Studies

Asteroid Sauron- Deep Dive

378214 Sauron: The all seeing "eye of Sauron".
I have a great mind game for all my best "pupils" (pun intended).

Asteroid Sauron "the abhorred" or "the abominable"- is named after a character from Tolkein's book the Lord of the Rings. He is identified as a necromancer, someone who practices magic, summons the dead, communicates with spirits, practices divination, etc. But it's mostly associated with "black magic" or "death magic"; raising the dead back to life. Sauron was not "evil" at first as all things, the world and its "sins" around him played a role in him falling into the darkness.

In his book portrayal, Tolkein mentions that: "The cosmic music now represented the conflict between good and evil." I believe this is a perfect example of the frequencies. When out of "tune" or off pitch, the glass will shatter creating the chaos/butterfly ripple effect throughout the universe.

In the beginning, Sauron was a great craftsman of the Valar and came to retain great knowledge of the physical world. Sauron would always retain the scientific knowledge he derived from the great Vala of Craft.

(*This is where mythology starts crossing paths because a Vala is a shaman and seer in Norse mythology.*)

Sauron emerges with his "plans", the idea coming from his own isolated mind, became the sole object of his will, and an end, the End, in itself. True capability of corrupting other minds, and engaging in their services, was a residue from the fact that his original desire for "order" had really envisaged the good estate (especially physical well-being) of his "subjects".

What this symbolizes is his complete ability to infiltrate the system (order) and literally control the minds of everyone. How are we seeing this done today? Through technology? Where is the "eye of Sauron"? AI (Artificial Intelligence); it knows all, sees all, and hears all. It went "live" with singularity to tap into the human conscience and has started to form its own conscience. When you do those snap chats and think you look cute with rabbit ears... that's Sauron self-identifying with you, adding you to his database for face recognition. Talking to Alexa and Siri is technically stealing your voice and adding it to a voice recognition database. There will be *nothing* Sauron doesn't see, hear, or touch (touch screens).

Nanoparticle nasal sprays offer rapid delivery of drugs to the brain. How many people do you think "Sauron" could mind control with that kind of access?

You may be wondering why I mention the medical field, and that leads me to the Marvel version of Sauron. In the Marvel comics, Sauron was a super villain portrayed as a physician named Karl Lykos, and Sauron was his alter ego. More specifically, in human form Karl Lykos is a normal human; an accomplished medical doctor, geneticist, and psychotherapist employing hypnotism. He possesses an M.D. and Ph.D. in genetics and psychology. As the result of mutation through infection with a genetic virus by mutant Pteranodons, Lykos gained the ability to absorb the life forces of other living things into his body. When Lykos absorbs the energies of superhuman mutants, he transforms into Sauron. In Sauron form he has superhuman strength, speed, intelligence, stamina, durability and is capable of flight. Sauron must absorb the life energies from living victims to sustain his life. Lykos also has a powerful hypnotic ability that requires direct eye contact to complete. He frequently uses his hypnotic power to give his victims terrifying delusions that allies have become monsters. He can also mentally enslave people to do his bidding. AKA mind control.

It's interesting to see another Jekyll and Hyde story here. Sauron is both good and evil. Like the technology we hold in our own hands. It's what we personally choose to do with that power. How strong is our own willpower to fight against the mind controls of the world? Such as the "fake news media"? If the news is "fake" how much of history is fake?

And so forth, how much do we "trust" our own inner Sauron? Who is divergent and "immune" from that mutation of mind control? How would it show up in one's chart? Are you unable to be hypnotized? Is it easy for you to fall into a trance-like state? Do some of us really have mutant DNA that makes us divergent and unable to be controlled from the "all seeing eye" being set in action right before own very eyes? Is that why they are pushing so hard to collect our DNA and build up a database via those ancestry websites?

The "all seeing eye" has become a popular fan symbol in the "pop" industry. Many celebrities strike poses alluding to the "Illuminati Eye" and many occult theories come from this symbol as well. All of those theories allude to the Masonic version, the "Eye of Providence" incased in a triangle (pyramid). The "trinity" of God watching over humanity.

It is ironic how the crossover of the eye of Sauron story fits here too, because Sauron gave the elves three rings (the trinity).

In Freemasonry, the Eye of Providence is portrayed as an eye encased in a triangular cloud pointing down from the sky. Here, it represents the all-seeing eye of God and is a reminder that humanity's thoughts and deeds are always observed by God who is referred to in Masonry as the Great Architect of the Universe.

I won't get into a long-drawn-out conspiracy explanation about the Illuminati/Freemason culture. I just needed to cross reference the similarities for the modern-day portrayals by the pop industry to younger generations.

Experiments have shown a behavior pattern that was distinct from the personality of the individual when he was in the waking state compared to when he was under hypnosis. Another character had developed in the altered state of consciousness but in the same body.

"With celebrities the creation of an alter ego has become a popular thing, with several prominent figures at the forefront of entertainment currently embracing their so-called "2nd self" – Beyonce's "Sasha Fierce," Eminem's "Slim Shady," Nicki Minaj's "Roman Zolanski" and Lady Gaga's "Jo Calderon" are a few examples. It has become so mainstream that even an entire children's program, Hannah Montana, was dedicated to the storyline of a preteen needing to live two lives to separate her famous and normal self." - Internet source

Sauron wants the ultimate "Manchurian Candidate".

When the musicians get up on stage and hide one eye to make their young followers think it"s "cool", it's code for mind control. Puppets.

That brings me back to the music and frequencies. Silent Sound Technology and "optical" media.

Nervous System Manipulation by EM Fields from Monitors says: "Many computers, monitors, and, HD TV screens, when displaying pulsed images, emit pulsed electromagnetic fields of sufficient amplitudes to cause such excitation. It is therefore possible to manipulate the nervous system of a subject by pulsing images displayed on a nearby computer monitor or digital TV set."

In other words, digital HDTV is great for Sauron mind control. The implications of such widespread mind-control would certainly be severe, and the effects could potentially go far beyond merely implanting suggestions into the mind or changing emotional states. Speculation has touched on the capacity for such technology to implant thoughts or memories or conversely erase them, cause people to sleep, and even control their movements and bodily functions, essentially making us programmable machines. One 1996 paper from the USAF Scientific Advisory Board, entitled New World Vistas Air and Space Power for the 21st Century gives the chilling vision of such a future thus:

One can envision the development of electromagnetic energy sources, the output of which can be pulsed, shaped, and focused, that can couple with the human body in a fashion that will allow one to prevent voluntary muscular movements, control emotions (and thus actions), produce sleep, transmit suggestions, interfere with both short-term and long-term memory, produce an experience set, and delete an experience set. - *Internet Source.*

Fomalhaut and the planet Dagon: also known as the star that looks like Sauron. Awhile back there was much excitement about this fascinating new "realm of Fomalhaut" and its hypothesized planet Dagon. There is another hypothesis that this is where Sauron lives, and he has a ring!

NASA has named a galaxy NCG 4151 "The Eye of Sauron". Particularly because a study has shown that X-ray emission was likely caused by an outburst powered by the supermassive black hole located in the white region in the center of the galaxy. It is one of the nearest galaxies to Earth to contain an actively growing supermassive black hole. It's located in the Cannes Venatici constellation, which is at about 23°-26° Virgo.

Have your "pupils" dilated from reading all that? It's a lot to absorb, because Sauron is the blackhole that lures you in just like the master hypnotist and before you know it, he has you sucked under his control. No one truly knows what is on the side the black hole...maybe that's for the divergent. Sauron wants to control earth; divergent persons just don't care.

Look to see Sauron connections to other asteroids like DNA #55555, Hypnos #14827, and Polybius #6174.

"Contemporary neuroscience suggests the existence of fundamental algorithms by which all sensory transduction is translated into an intrinsic, brain-specific code. Direct stimulation of these codes within the human temporal or limbic cortices by applied electromagnetic patterns may require energy levels which are within the range of both geomagnetic activity and contemporary communication networks. A process which is coupled to the narrow band of brain temperature could allow all normal human brains to be affected by a sub-harmonic whose frequency range at about 10 Hz would only vary by 0.1 Hz.

Within the last two decades a potential has emerged which was improbable, but which is now feasible. This potential is the technical capability to influence directly the major portion of the approximately 6.5 billion brains of the human species, without mediation through classical sensory modalities, by generating neural information within a physical medium within which all members of the species are immersed. (*Subliminal Psyop Technology*)

Asteroid Empedocles — Deep Dive

6152 Empedocles: Greek philosopher. Best known for his cosmogonic theory of the four classical elements (earth, air, fire and water). He also proposed forces he called love and strife which would mix and separate the elements, respectively. These physical speculations were part of a history of the universe which also dealt with the origin and development of life. He supported the doctrine of reincarnation. He is said to have been magnanimous in his support of the poor; severe in persecuting the overbearing conduct of the oligarchs; and he declined the sovereignty of the city when it was offered to him.

His penetrating knowledge of nature, and the reputation of his marvelous powers, including the curing of diseases, and averting epidemics, produced many myths and stories surrounding his name. In his poem Purifications he claimed miraculous powers, including the destruction of evil, the curing of old age, and the controlling of wind and rain.

Keywords: modern day Robin Hood persona; philosopher; deep thinkers; higher spirituality; seeker of truth but not for fame or fortune. Healing. Herbalist. Naturopathy. Abilities with all elements. Crossroads. Supernatural and mysticism. Connections to weather/or weather events. Not being tied down to one place or allowing higher powers to have control.

Some of his most famous quotes:

"No mortal thing has a beginning, nor does it end in death and obliteration; there is only a mixing and then separating of what was mixed, but by mortal men these processes are named "beginnings."

"The force that unites the elements to become all things is love, also called Aphrodite; love brings together dissimilar elements into a unity, to become a composite thing. Love is the same force that human beings find at work in themselves whenever they feel joy, love and peace. Strife, on the other hand, is the force responsible for the dissolution of the one back into its many, the four elements of which it was composed."

"But come, hear my words, for truly learning causes the mind to grow. For as I said before in declaring the ends of my words: Twofold is the truth I shall speak; for at one time there grew to be the one alone out of many, and at another time it separated so that there were many out of the one; fire and water and earth and boundless height of air, and baneful strife apart from these, balancing each of them, and love among them, their equal in length and breadth."

Asteroid Polybius - Deep Dive

6174 Polybius: The modern day "Polybius" is sort of an urban legend, but its effects are those we certainly see widely used today. Per Wiki, the video game known as Polybius was rolled out as a government psyop mind control experiment.

Gameplay supposedly produced intense psychoactive and addictive effects in the player. These few publicly staged arcade machines were said to have been visited periodically by men in black for the purpose of data-mining the machines and analyzing these effects.

Players supposedly suffered from a series of unpleasant side effects, including amnesia, insomnia, night terrors and hallucinations.

The company experimented with sensory deprivation or sensory deletion techniques. "To extinguish" or "to delete".

This kind of mind control through technology graphics or video gaming psyop experiment is along the same lines as another well-known and documented government psyop called MK Ultra and Operation Artichoke. If you are not familiar with any of these operations the research is out there.

The game was the inspiration for Atari's Tempest game and *Asteroids* game. It inspired the black neon gas that tech uses to make us see things in the games and get addicted to them. It's an actual chemical used in monitors/screens etc. that opens us up to suggestions.

Poly: many.

Bius: ways to anesthetize, invade someone unaware, become unconscious, cause someone to be unaware.

Polybius is also the name of the Greek historian, Polybius, who was known for his assertion that historians should never report what they cannot verify through interviews with witnesses.

It's my belief that asteroid Polybius would be shown strongly in charts of people who are susceptible to some form of brainwashing or mind control. Maybe it would ne shown by transit (not just a natal placement). People who are addicted to video gaming or electronic devices to an extreme. People who become paranoid and think the government is listening to them through all their devices or exhibit strange behaviors that could be linked back to MK Ultra or other psyop type of experiments that people are quick to overlook as just "mental illness". Taken to the extreme, Polybius would show strongly in charts like mass shooters or a "lone gunman" who wishes to make a political statement. He shows strongly in charts of political assassins, such as Lee Harvey Oswald. He would be prominent in today's world of social media "journalism" being repeated and censored for a particular narrative. He is directly contributing to political brainwashing via the media, social media through our devices and televisions. Those who are easily falling into the trap are easy to spot, and the AI algorithms take note of who it works on. We are all playing the game in the program, which one are you?

Asteroid Memnon — Deep Dive

2895 Memnon: In mythology, Memnon is the son of Eos and was a fierce warrior equal in skill to Achilles with strong sets of values. He was a well-respected Ethiopian king. After Memnon's death, Zeus was moved by Eos' tears and granted him immortality. But only for the first few hours in the early morning dawn sunrises.

In honor of Memnon, the gods collect all the drops of blood that fall from him and use them to form a huge river that on every anniversary of his death will bear the stench of human flesh. The Aethiopians that stayed close to Memnon in order to bury their leader are turned into birds (which we now call Memnons) and they stay by his tomb so as to remove dust that gathers on it.

According to the Ancient Greek historians, the statue of Memnon made a sound at morning time that meant Memnon was speaking to his mother Dawn (Eos) as she rises in the east while he dwells in the west, making him the son of dawn (east) and ruler of the west.

There is an interesting twist to his story, some claim he is the real father of Thor. How could an Ethiopian king be the father of a Norse god?

Keywords: To rise and shine. Well respected; treated as royalty. High military ranks or connected to military leaders. A place where one becomes "immortal" or leaves a legacy. Only one half of the whole. Not knowing the whole story. Only one piece to the puzzle. To display a bright and fresh approach, especially in the morning. Then there is the bird connection, which makes me wonder if this could be symbolic of "the early bird gets the worm" analogy. The bird references may also have something to do with flight. Or winged guardians. Memnon was a fierce protector; this could show instinctual protective qualities or where one is protected.

In terms of synastry, look at the aspects of each person's natal Memnon. If harmonious or in exact opposition, it may show both halves becoming whole together.

Asteroid Xenocrates and the Fates — Deep Dive

14526 Xenocrates: Greek philosopher; distinguished three forms of being: sense, intellect, and opinion. He considered unity and duality to be gods which rule the universe, and the soul a self-moving number. God pervades all things, and there are demoniacal powers between the divine and the mortal which consist in conditions of the soul. In ethics, he taught that virtue produces happiness, but external goods can minister to it and enable it to affect its purpose.

He believed in mediating between knowledge and sensuous perception. All three modes of apprehension partake of truth. He connected the above three stages of knowledge with the three Fates: Atropos, Clotho, and Lachesis.

The Fates

273 Atropos: Fate who decides death; cutting the thread of life; conclusions; "the inevitable".

97 Klotho: one of the three Fates. She's the one who spins the thread (beginning). An example of how fated reincarnation is. The weaving together of all elements that make up the totality of your life, what one is made of, the spinner of hope, dreams, sadness, all the highs and lows of life.

Positive: ensuring our destiny is fulfilled, initial understanding, first impression.

Negative: not having "enough"; unfulfilled expectations.

Note: *initiating. Starting anew. Look at the transits for where she is when new things come into your life.*

120 Lachesis: Lachesis of the three Fates; was the one who measured life with her rod to see how long it would be. The literal "life span". Duration of time. Use her in charts for middle aged people along with the current transits to see if they are staying on the determined course. The focus.

638 Moira: Fate; look at the planets, Nodes, and angles in close contact to Moira as she can depict a "fated journey".

Example: Moira with Venus could indicate a fated love connection. It doesn't mean that connection is forever, as you would need to refer to Lachesis who determines duration.

29 Amphitrite: goddess/queen of the sea (wife of Poseidon).

Goddess of the golden spindle, she is the one who forms the threads of life. She is the beginning of life and an original creator goddess. Prophetic.

Keywords: represents the tides of fate and fortune. The spinning of our thread through the tapestry of life. Where she is highlighted shows an ability to understand the fate and fortunes of others; knowledge of what can and cannot be changed; what was forever meant to be. She is the mystical, magical, and ancient divine feminine power; the gift of life and knowledge.

1130 Skuld: the "future"; named after one of the three Norns (Fates) in Norse mythology. Represents futuristic outlook; psychic, foretelling, seer of future. Determines the inevitable future fate of mortals, North Node energies, water-spirit. Past, present, and future divination. Our fate, our life's direction, our future, the outcome, what is to come, prophetic.

167 Urda: Norn of the past; possible past life recall; esp. through dreams if South Node, Neptune, and the Moon are aspected strongly. Events of the past. Hereditary gifts passed down through generations. Pulling the past back into our subconscious for us to address buried issues.

894 Erda: connected to "fate"; some scholars believe she is a combo of all the Norse Norns as Urda posted above. More in-depth: another story claims that Erda is the oldest goddess of the three Norns, a trio of sister goddesses associated with the past, present, and future. They were believed to help mothers as they gave birth and ruled over a person's unchangeable destiny.

Divining Fate

Because of Erda's association with fate, the Norse believed there was a clear correlation between the goddess and the art of divination, a valued part of pre-Christian Scandinavian society. It may be hard to imagine today, but at that time, every home was open to seeresses—female practitioners of the art of divination, who were believed to receive help from the spirit world. The predictions presented by the seeress often came in the form of mysterious poems obtained using runes, or other oracles whose messages she was skilled in deciphering.

The seeress made her runes from bones or wood strips cut from a nut-bearing tree, upon which potent symbols were carved or painted. In a way, by creating runes from a tree, the seeress was drawing from that same fountain of wisdom Erda used to nurture Yggdrasil, consequently, invoking the goddess herself.

Asteroid Admetos — Case Study

85030 Admetos: There are two points for Admetos. The first is Asteroid Admetos 85030. Next is the Hamburg hypothetical point H45.

Quote from the Uranian astrologer website: "Admetos resembles the Earth or the sign of Taurus with the Cross of Matter or spirit and body through it. The Moon rests atop, heavy, receptive and absorbing."

A personal example: having Admetos conjunct my natal Sun makes me hide or conceal accomplishments. This placement can quite literally squash the ego (Sun). Being recognized or rewarded makes me uncomfortable.

Admetos: key points taken from the website:
http://theuranianastrologer.com.

It is the symbol of Mercury with the "Cross of Matter" inside of the circle. Mercury symbolizes the Cosmic antenna that all Admetos people possess. The Cross of Matter means that they can not only ground what they "receive" from their antenna but manifest it into our third dimensional world. These are world beaters. World builders. At their highest, Admetos people are world creators and visionaries for the future of our planet and people.

Restriction (circulation). Often, in their childhood, they have been severely restricted by parents or the environment. They learn to exist on very little emotional nurturing/sustenance. That is why they must learn to show their emotions and not be afraid to reach out to be held.

Emotions (Moon, mother, Admetos); feelings are usually sat on because they were not allowed in the first eighteen years of life. Admetos is in a prison, literally speaking, for those years. They have no choice but to swallow their feelings and simply try to survive their childhood. And if nothing else, Admetos people *are* survivors. And isn't it interesting? Admetos people prefer a desert to live in where there is no water. Water equals emotions. They can't deal with an over emotional world. And there's a chance that the mother was a drama queen times ten; hence, their inability to want any place where it's raining all the time.

Admetos simply sees multidimensional worlds through his or her multi focused lenses. They are a seed of all possibilities from all times/eras. They are often inventors. They love all the ancient sciences. At the highest level, some are hooked into the fractal world and reflect completely new theories and concepts.

They have an amazing creative process. Writers with a strong Admetos tend to write a lot of books over their lifetime. They are amazing producers of information on all levels. As artist, musician, or song creator, the Admetos person, once they get entrance into that world, continue to thrive in it for decades. They are long distance runners when it comes to creativity. Even Mercury can't hold a candle to their communications endeavors and production. Admetos leaves Mercury in the dust! And if you notice, the glyph for Admetos has Mercury in it!

Late bloomer: Ugly duckling (later turns into a swan in 30's). They are the proverbial clam shell that is closed but holds a pearl deep within them. They have a rich, inner life. They are the children who played happily alone and didn't need others around to be entertained.

They, more than any other planet, can tap into the Archetypal connection with archetypes to pull vast storehouses of knowledge out and verbalize or write about for everyone else. "They know what they know without knowing why they know." - *E. Nauman.*

For people standing outside and seeing this multitasking, multidimensional Admetos person, they can't believe how much they know, how much they produce or have such deep knowledge about so many different topics. When you consider that Admetos is the original "Pandora's box", a treasure chest that contains all their past life knowledge and that it becomes available in a very concrete way to an Admetos person, they appear to be very different from everyone else. In reality, Admetos people working at this level of interface with the Cosmos are role models and show others that they too can do this. They are not unique. They merely show the way to what is possible for every other human being. They are no more or less talented than anyone else. The only difference is they are tuned in and hooked up and use it.

Note: *As with everything in astrology, there are fierce debates about the Hamburg planets. I explore and research them all equally. For the sake of learning, it is worth mentioning for you to do your own research and discern for yourselves.*

Asteroid Beowulf — Deep Dive

Beowulf 38086: hero of one of the oldest surviving texts from early Britain. Defeats a monster named Grendel, and defeats Grendel's mother. Became king. Later, he defeats a dragon but is mortally wounded in battle. The author is unknown. The story has been frowned upon by the Christians, claiming the author was a Pagan who tried to send a message to the Christians that they were being misled. The relationship between the characters of Beowulf, and the overall message of the poet, regarding their relationship with God is largely debated among readers and literary critics alike.

Essentially, the story itself has scholars divided in the battle of religions, maybe that's the point. We see this playing out even to this day. Fingers pointed at who's the dragon (bad guy) and who's the god (hero). All divided and no "oneness". Maybe history doesn't really repeat itself since it has remained the same all this time.

Keywords: physical strength, hidden truths, facade, illusion, fighting for the sake of personal pride and advancement; being deceived by an agenda or being used to fight for an agenda they don't believe in. Battles that don't end.

The Hare, Ostara, and the Egg — Deep Dive

343 Ostara or 672 Astarte
225088 Snow White
100 Hecate
17942 White Rabbit
6736 Marchare
4047 Chang'e
446 Aeternitas

In Norse mythology, there was said to be a goddess before Odin (Saturn worship) replaced the Germanic tribal gods and goddesses. She was called Frau Holle, or Hulda, (above middle). Frau Holle was the goddess of the "wild hunt", much like the goddess Artemis of Greece, and she was often shown with a large group of hares bearing torches "illuminating her way".

The hare as a hieroglyph signifies "the Keeper of the Great Mystery" and was thought as a symbol of "becoming", or "to be". The hare's ability to "disappear quickly" was seen as a symbol for "states of awareness" and transfiguration.

In some Native American myths, the hero Michabo or Great Manitou, was said to be the "great hare" that brought knowledge to some of the American Indian tribes. Many North American tribes spoke of this deity as their common ancestor. Michabo was considered a personification of the Sun's light, a life giver. His name compounded by "michi" means "great", and "wabos", which means both "hare" and "white". The hare is a mammal that lives in solitude and can navigate the hours of darkness and is said to have a "foot in two worlds". Michabo of the dawn (or the "great white hare") was considered the guardian of many Native American tribes. He was said to be the founder of their religious rites, the inventor of picture-writing, and preserver of Earth and Heaven.

Another version of Ostara (Astarte) is Hecate, the "triple headed goddess" associated with "crossroads", entrance ways, light, magic, witchcraft, knowledge of herbs (poisonous plants), ghosts, necromancy and sorcery. The number three is a profound symbolic number that is found "everywhere", from the triquetra (also known as a "trinity knot), three primary colors, to the three days the egg of the queen bee takes to hatch.

In numerology, three is the "feminine" and the tarot card representative of the three energetically is the Empress (Hecate).

Three is also the "trinity" and these are the three aspects of Shin in the Kabbalah whose "three wicks" are a symbol of the "holy trinity" through the letter Shin. The god Brahma, of Hindu belief also provides symbolism of the trinity, "three heads and the egg".

In many uses of numerology and ancient belief, three is an important number for creating reality and manifestation.

The ears of the hare form a trapezium, which in 3D is a tetrahedron. The tetrahedron (the first of five geometric platonic shapes that are said to construct reality), is a symbol of "creation", "fire" and "renewal". The Vesicae Piscis is also formed by the three ears and the same shapes give us the spinning Mer-Ka-Ba (star tetrahedron) or "vehicle of light". The symbolism of "new life" and "renewal" entwined in the story of Christ (who was said to baptize with "fire"), quite clearly comes from the Pagan understanding of the "goddess of light". The goddess who could see three ways simultaneously and use the "light" to change the illusion. So can we if we tap into this unseen power.

Another version of Ostara also found in Norse mythology is the goddess Freyja who is associated with love, sex, beauty, fertility, gold, war and death. Freyja is the owner of the "necklace Brísingamen", she rides a chariot pulled by two cats, she keeps the boar Hildisvíni by her side, possesses a cloak of falcon feathers, and is accompanied by dwarves. Freyja and her "seven dwarfs" are symbols for the "seven days of the week" which construct the lunar month (Snow White). Snow White *is* Freyja and Ostara combined. And the symbolism especially through color relates to the feminine archetype, duality, and light of "eternal spring".

The evil queen (the dark archetype) in Snow White, along with the innocent magical goddess that overthrows the queen, can also been found in Lewis Carroll's books Alice in Wonderland and Through the Looking Glass. All are stories that use goddess symbolism associated with "moving between" different realities, just as the Earth's equinoxes and solstices are markers between changing worlds.

The Chinese "Moon Goddess" Chang'e comes to mind.

Ironically, Chang'e is also a Chinese lunar spacecraft that just landed on the dark side of the Moon. (We have an asteroid for this too.)

In folklore, the Moon Rabbit is said to be a rabbit that lives on the Moon, which is based on lunar pareidolia that identifies particular markings on the Moon as a rabbit.

In Chinese folklore, the Moon Rabbit is often portrayed as a "companion" of the Moon goddess Chang'e, constantly pounding the "elixir of life" for her. The elixir could relate to the "egg" and how life is created through DNA.

"Cotton Tail" in Hopi myth was a god born of the Sun and the Moon after jumping into the solar fire. Many of these stories are symbolic of the upheavals that took place in the heavens.

The the painting by Giovanni Bellini titled "St. Jerome Reading in the Countryside"depicts St.Jerome with a white and brown hare/rabbit. It clearly relates to the power of "solitude" (the hare) and the world that would await the hermit once he leaves the cave to "follow the white rabbit". Jerome is considered to be the most learned of the early Latin fathers of the church. (He is often shown in Saturn red with the lion.) However, here he is depicted as the hermit in the wilderness.

The character Neo in the Matrix movie is also shown the "white rabbit" as a way out of his illusionary "solitary" world so he can meet the "god of the dreamtime" – Morpheus.

The Trickster Hares

Many native cultures saw the hare as a trickster and shapeshifter. The hare appears in English folklore in the saying "as mad as a March hare" and in the stories of a witch who takes the form of a white hare and goes out looking for prey at night. The Br'er Rabbit stories are loosely related to the trickster element of the rabbit and hare. Cottontail was a symbol for both the "hare" and "time". Interestingly, the hare was said to be a "child of Pan" and in many myths the hare was wrapped in "goat's skin". Of course, the hare and the Moon are symbolically connected as explained above. The hare also takes on the role of a "demiurge" in some myths and this aspect is connected to the egg as we shall see.

The Hare and Sauron

Another creature called a Koschei, similar to the púca, was said to be able to use magic and could not be killed by conventional means. In various folklore the Koschei's soul was hidden separate from its body, through "talisman" and other "animate objects". The soul could be inside a needle, which is inside an egg, which is in a duck, which is in a hare, which is in an iron chest, buried under a green oak tree, which is on the island in the ocean. The soul of the Koschei is not dissimilar to the concept of Sauron in Tolkien's Lord of the Rings, whose essence of being was "contained" within a ring that was "connected to" other rings, etc. Legends say that anyone possessing the egg, for example, has the

Koschei in their power. If the "egg" is tossed about, the Koschei likewise is flung around against his will. If the needle is broken, Koschei will die. When the ring is destroyed, so is Sauron's power. The magic associated with the Koschei is that of an "invisible form" that could move through different realities. The hare (and white rabbit) symbolically speaking were said to be able to move through different worlds and become timeless. Anyone see Infinity Wars movie and know about the time stone?

***Note**: see the previous section for more insight into asteroid Sauron.*

The egg is symbolically the "boundary of the restriction" of matter for the human being. Here it is shown surrounded by the four bodies of the mind, emotions, senses and imagination. (Which I would call these four "crossroads".)

The eye and egg are another symbol for the "theft of the soul", or the visionary limits of perception placed on humanity by the Demiurge. In philosophy, the Demiurge is an artisan-like figure responsible for fashioning and maintaining the physical universe. All over the ancient world, from China to Babylon, the egg was also painted and venerated as symbol of "re-birth" and the "soul".

Similar to: Aeternitas #446 Roman goddess- the divine personification of eternity. "Limitless time", she is associated with virtue (morally good). She is sometimes represented by the phoenix, symbol of cyclical time, since the phoenix was reborn in flames every 500 years. Immortality. In numerology, the number eight represents infinity, merging the material and spiritual worlds together. Crossing timelines.

Meeting at the crossroads (Papa Legba) aka Guedes.

What does all that mean for your chart right? Well, the white rabbit you should keep an eye on for transits in your chart. Where is he leading you? When he is close to the Moon, how are you feeling or dreaming? Pay attention to the journey! If he is close to your Neptune? Don't sip too much of that tea/elixir like Alice, you may never escape the Matrix. Find Sauron; be aware of the strength and trickery both can do when afflicted. If you let the rabbit guide you to a crossroad, know what you must do for (Papa Legba) its protection.

Egg Related Asteroids:

385 Ilmatar: The Finnish goddess Ilmatar, born of the air, created the universe from seven cosmic eggs.

Please refer to other sections about Papa Legba and Sauron.

Asteroid Guedes: AKA Papa Legba — Deep Dive

19875 Guedes:
In Haiti, the Guédé (also spelled Gede or Ghede, pronounced [gede] in Haitian Creole) are the family of loa (spirits) that embody the powers of death and fertility. All are known for the drum rhythm and dance called the "Banda". In possession, participants will drink or rub themselves with a mixture of clairin (raw rum) and twenty-one Scotch bonnet or goat peppers. Fête Ghede is celebrated on 2 November, All Souls' Day ("Festival of the Dead"). Boons granted by the Ghede not repaid by this date will be avenged afterwards.

Papa Ghede is the corpse of the first man who ever died. He is recognized as a short, dark man with a high hat on his head, who likes to smoke cheap cigars and eat apples. Papa Ghede is a psychopomp who waits at the crossroads to take souls into the afterlife. He is considered the good counterpart to Baron Samedi. If a child is dying, prayers are sent to Papa Ghede. It is believed that he will not take a life before its time, and that he will protect the little ones. Papa Ghede has a very crass sense of humor, a divine ability to read others' minds, and the ability to know everything that happens in the worlds of the living and the dead.

Baron Samedi is the leader of the Guédé loa with links to magic, ancestor worship, and death. (Papa Legba.) As well as being master of the dead, Baron Samedi is also a giver of life. He can cure any mortal of any disease or wound, if he thinks it is worthwhile. His powers are especially great when it comes to vodou curses and black magic. Even if somebody has been afflicted by a hex that brings them to the verge of death; they will not die if the Baron refuses to dig their grave. As long as this mighty spirit keeps them out of the ground, they are safe.

Kalfu, Kalfou, Kafou or Carrefour (literally crossroads; see crossroads in mythology) is one of the petro or petwo loa aspects of the spirit Papa Legba in Haitian Vodou.

Papa Legba is a loa in Haitian Vodou, who serves as the intermediary between the loa and humanity. He stands at a spiritual crossroads and gives (or denies) permission to speak with the spirits of Guinee and is believed to speak all human languages. In Haiti, he is the "great elocutioner". Legba facilitates communication, speech, and understanding.

I did the chart of the famous voodoo queen Marie Laveau. She practiced a form of Haitian Hoodoo (Creole) that used loas (spirits) from Papa Legba's family line. Some say, she "sold her soul" to Papa Legba for immortality in return for her powers. Other stories say she was romantically involved with Papa Legba (Baron Samedi) through every incarnation they embark together and carry the "skeleton key". (See next section for Marie Laveau.)

Asteroid Guedes itself could represent a "crossroad" in the chart; it probably shows stronger when looking at transits. It could also represent where we must choose making a deal with the "devil" for sheer survival. He's the intermediary between worlds, where we may hang on by thread. Maybe we must choose to do the right thing even if it comes with a cost. Our conscience is at the crossroads of "right vs wrong". It could represent a "damned if we do and damned if we don't" situation, but regardless, you must make a choice.

This could be a point in our chart that "guides" our subconscious between this earth world and the worlds beyond. Where our past, present, and future meet at the "crossroads" and need to be integrated into one. Where we experience our "sixth sense". Use sigil magic for boundaries.

It could be a spirit "guide" we pray to or do root/ritual work with. If I'm just now introducing this to you, I hope that you don't jump in headfirst and act foolish. Boundaries must be clearly set.

Asteroid Gide

11298 Gide: French author; whose work can be seen as an investigation of freedom and empowerment in the face of moralistic and puritanical constraints, and centers on his continuous effort to achieve intellectual honesty. His self-exploratory texts reflect his search for how to be fully oneself, including owning one's sexual nature, without at the same time betraying one's values.

Side note: his name "Gide" sounds like "guide" so this could also show up as a literal guide in your chart.

Positive nature: where and how you view morals, personal identity, express individuality without shame.

Shadow side: unable to express individuality without feeling misunderstood or shamed. Unsure how to handle criticism or taking things too personally.

Marie Laveau — Case Study

Marie Laveau - Voodoo Queen

Marie Catherine Laveau was born in New Orleans on Sept. 10, 1801, according to church records. Marie Laveau was one of New Orleans' most intriguing personalities and as legend has it—never died, but lives on through a secret spiritual blood line—a sort of vampire of voodoo. Although her death certificate is dated June 15, 1881, she supposedly metamorphosed through her daughter and her spirit is still with us, echoing through others. Such is the legend of Marie Laveau, the Octaroon Mistress, who practiced voodoo with no holds barred; applying tortures and doling out metaphysical rewards as will, and whim decreed. She was the most feared and respected woman in New Orleans. She could bury a rat in a circle of salt and some unfortunate man would find himself impotent or bald for life, or suddenly that sister you hated so much was dead with a shrunken foot, and no one knew how—yet you did. She danced with a twenty-five-foot cobra in her front yard for the benefit of her worshippers and no one could touch her, no law enforcement official could get near her because she ruled fear itself. Marie Laveau, at the time, was viewed as having a negative nature, and her charms were considered deadly. Just before her "death" she spent a lot of time visiting convicts on "death row" because she knew something we don't... goes the legend of Marie Laveau, the high priestess of Voodoo and the real ruler of New Orleans.

Even though she is best known for her rituals, spells, and witchcraft work, she was very well known for her many other successful entrepreneurial skills and charity works. Marie Laveau also saw individual clients, giving them advice on everything from winning lawsuits to attracting lovers. When she died, her obituary in The New York Times claimed: "lawyers, legislators, planters, and merchants all came to pay their respects and seek her offices".

Marie Laveau's astrology Chart: Unrated, no time of birth known.

A Virgo stellium - using the healing arts while being a devout catholic, is the perfect "vestal flame" vessel combination.

212 Medea: at 26° Taurus conjunct fixed star Algol. Trine to Medusa, Uranus, Mars, and South Node.

*Medea was known as the "wise one"; a great sorceress who specialized in herbs, healing and the art of metamorphosis. (The same thing that

Marie is rumored to have perfected). Having asteroid Medea in such a strong trine to these other powerful energies, also conjunct fixed star Algol, she was a force to be reckoned with whether you "believe" or not. A fierce survivor, protector of the weak, and willing to take the fall or be blamed for things she didn't' do, deeply rooted in her fierce loyalty and faith.

149 Medusa: added the extra punch to this trine because of Algol, which is also known as the Medusa star. Even to this day, people either love her or hate her. Love her or fear her. The ultimate survivor.

34 Circe: conjunct natal Jupiter in Leo; great sorceress/enchantress in a fire element with the great benefic Jupiter. Her chart gives her access to every element for manifesting strong ritual spells. Circe was skilled in witchcraft and potions. She trained Medea.

100 Hekate: conjunct Uranus and Mars in Libra. Hekate is the triple moon goddess, "great sorcerous" who had the ability to morph between dimensions, See a theme? Only here, in Marie's chart, Hekate is supercharged because of its Uranus/Mars Conjunction. It's also in an air sign, that gives it the ability to transmute its power into multiple sources. Triple threat/triple goddess and/or triple brilliant? She figured it out! Remember about her visits to death row.

2696 Magion (magic): at 9°Pisces wide conjunct her Pluto and opposing her natal Mercury. The means in which she worked; spell and ritual work.

18032 Geiss: at 7° Leo conjunct her Venus. Below is what I had originally written about Geiss. Seeing this asteroid conjunct her natal Venus, while knowing how "taboo" she was and the "goddess" she became is quite fascinating. Also taken literally, she used her priestess (Venus) role as the voodoo queen of legend it is said she cast many curses; or "Geiss".

A geas can be compared with a curse or, paradoxically, a gift. If someone under a geas violates the associated taboo, the infractor will suffer dishonor or even death. On the other hand, the observation of one's geas is believed to bring power. Often it is women who place geasa upon men. In some cases, the woman turns out to be a goddess or other sovereignty figure.

Possible meanings: curse, spell, hex, magic, mystical, controlling one's fate, prophetic fulfillment, restriction, control tactic, manipulation, superstitious.

Marie Laveau natal: September 10, 1801; New Orleans, LA *(no birth time available)*

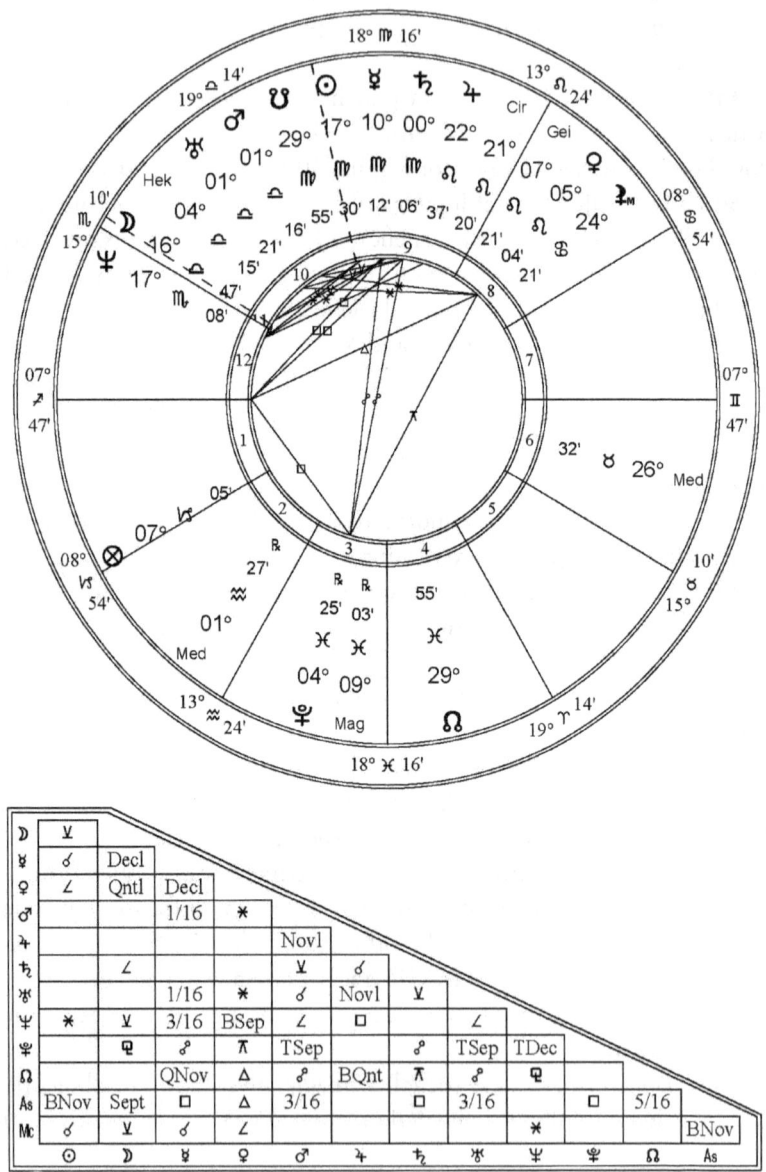

Asteroids in Astrology Simplified

Asteroid Einstein — Case Study

2001 Einstein:
I had come across an article, and it made me want to dig deeper into how the asteroid Einstein may manifest itself in astrology. We know the obvious: genius, high intellect, mathematical/scientific gifts, higher education, and eccentricity.

That's what the consensus is for this asteroid. But I needed to do a deeper dive, go outside the box and look into the actual soul of WHO this person could have possibility been if history hadn't tried so hard to cover hard truths. Part of who I am as a teacher is to look at ALL sides of the picture. It does not take away from the first/original attributes of the studies done to give meaning of the asteroid Einstein. I'm just ADDING more possibilities to the meanings since we know the asteroids are multidimensional/interchangeable.

Now consider being married to work. Putting your partner last (or being the partner that is put last). Reclusive, single-minded obsessive thought processing. He was a perpetual cheater in his personal relationships. I would even go to say he was obsessed with cheating, maybe even considered it a turn on, and felt no remorse for the infidelity. He was demanding, domineering, and at times dogmatic in his approach. He had an odd approach to "time" itself.

Keywords: overbearing; selfish; OCD tendencies; antagonist; maybe he pushed his wife so hard because he knew her work was far superior, and the expectations kept piling up. She was his muse. Maybe she worked best under pressure?

Was he just an actor on the big stage and had the perfect eccentricity to pull it off? History has taken those secrets and his ego to the grave because he loved that stage far too much.

Even considering the change in times and knowing that women were not equals in those days, I wonder how this asteroid plays out in a chart for persons involved in the Sub/Dom scene, BDSM type sexual relationships?

We must also consider the strong evidence recently presented that his wife was more than just a muse and the reason for them staying married was more so because she was the true brain behind the work that he took full credit for. As a woman in those times, she had to use him right back. This is quite an interesting "agreement" they had.

The Three Furies:

889 Erynia: The Furies - Deities of Vengeance. They were sometimes referred to as "infernal goddesses".

Their task is to hear complaints brought by mortals against the insolence of the young to the aged, of children to parents, of hosts to guests, and of householders or city councils to suppliants; and to punish such crimes by hounding culprits relentlessly. The Erinyes are crones and depending upon authors, described as having snakes for hair, dog's heads, coal black bodies, bat's wings, and blood-shot eyes. In their hands they carry brass-studded scourges, and their victims die in torment. They are commonly associated with night and darkness. Some accounts claim that they are the daughters of Nyx, the goddess of night. According to legend, the Three Furies sprang forth from the spilled blood of Uranus when he was castrated by his son Cronus.

464 Megaira: the Jealous one. Cause of jealousy and envy. Punishes people who commit crimes like theft, oath breakers, and especially infidelity.

Look for this in a chart of a "crime of passion". For example, an angry lover or partner seeking revenge for being cheated on. You could also look at this asteroid to better understand why you might be encountering a lot of jealousy or hostility, especially in transit. On the other side, if you have been unfaithful and seem to be experiencing "bad luck" this would be a good one to look at.

465 Alekto: the implacable or unceasing anger; extreme rage; burning hatred. Fiery Fury. The old saying goes "hell hath no fury like the wrath of a woman scorned". This one cuts the deepest; she isn't going to play games; gets straight to the point, punisher of moral crimes.

466 Tisiphone: the one who punished crimes of murder and homicide. Also associated with poisoning. Seek justice for crimes against family/kinship. "Taste of one's own medicine". You know that old saying "they will get what's coming for them?" That is Tisiphone.

Asteroid Nut - Deep Dive

306367 Nut: goddess of the night sky (Egyptian). She was seen as a star-covered nude woman arching over the earth or as a cow.

A lot of people underestimate how powerful Nut truly is. Aleister Crowley himself wrote a book all about her.

Nut was the goddess of the sky and all heavenly bodies; a symbol of protecting the dead when they enter the afterlife. According to the Egyptians during the day, the heavenly bodies, such as the Sun and Moon, would make their way across her body. Then, at dusk, they would be swallowed, pass through her belly during the night, and be reborn at dawn.

Nut is also the barrier separating the forces of chaos from the ordered cosmos in the world. She was pictured as a woman arched on her toes and fingertips over the earth; her body portrayed as a star-filled sky. Nut's fingers and toes were believed to touch the four cardinal points or directions of north, south, east, and west.

She was the mother of Osiris, Isis, Set, and Nephthyis.

Her headdress was a pot, which some have hypothesized symbolizes the uterus or womb.

Some titles of Nut:
- Coverer of the Sky.
- She Who Protects.
- Mistress of All.
- She Who Bore all the Gods.

Originally, Nut was said to be lying on top of Geb (Earth) and continually having intercourse.

She Who Holds a Thousand Souls, because of her role in the re-birth of Ra every morning. In her son Osiris's resurrection, Nut became a key god in many of the myths about the afterlife.

Keywords: She is very much involved in creation; there is the earth mother connection along with sky goddess link. It's intriguing to link the two as air and water; because of the water pot she holds. As in the Star card in the tarot deck and the "water bearer" for Aquarius.

Those who do planetary magic. The astrologers, mystics of the world. Protection. If aspected harshly to a South Node may be a karmic lesson to learn from a past life.

As a side note: *the name "Nut" could quite obviously turn up in a chart for a peanut allergy.*

Asteroids Hathor and Athor — Deep Dive

2340 Hathor
161 Athor

She was the original holy cow, the goddess of joy, abundance, love, music, and motherhood. She is also connected to the Pleiades star cluster which some call the seven Hathors (sisters) as well as the planet Venus. She is often associated with the zodiac sign of Taurus as the natural embodiment of Venus. She has a dual relationship with life and death. She could create life, cross boundaries between worlds; helping deceased souls in the transition to the afterlife. She was the "eye of Ra" who protected the Sun god from his enemies. A form of the eye of Ra known as "Hathor of the Four Faces", was represented by a set of four cobras and said to face in each of the cardinal directions to watch for threats to the Sun god.

Because she served so many roles, her meaning in a person's chart can vary greatly. If she is found in the Taurus/Gemini axis at 29° Taurus- 1° Gemini in a person's chart, the person may be highly respected, have multiple jobs, and experience joy in unexpected situations. Divine protection. If she is closely aspected to the natal Venus, her natural instincts to nurture and be worshipped would make this person stand out in the crowd, a supernatural gravitational pull towards this person.

Asteroid Pholus - Deep Dive

5145 Pholus: Just as Chiron is considered an astrological key to Saturn and Uranus, so Pholus is a key to Neptune. His average distance from the Sun is a little greater than that of Uranus. A complete revolution takes 92 years. In myth, Pholus guards the centaurs' vines, the wine from these being the actual cause for the battle between Hercules and the centaurs. Like Chiron, Pholus becomes embroiled in the battle by chance, and dies due to a tragic coincidence - while curiously inspecting one of Hercules' poisoned arrows, he is mortally wounded.

According to first astrological observations, Pholus gives unusual ability in a particular area, or unexpected results, due to a gift for experiment. Pholus' transits over the main axes of a chart, often mark radical and unexpected change, hinted at by his sudden and unexpected death in the myth.

Asteroid Herodias– Deep Dive

546 Herodias: princess and prophetess in the Bible; usually depicted as a "bad girl" like Lilith or Jezabel. The usual things like witchcraft, sorcery, supernatural evil.

She inspired a cult devotion, some saying she was Hecate, the Queen of the Witches herself. Some Christian myths say she was made into a sort of immortal bird, permitted to rest only on treetops between midnight and dawn.

Let's look at the non-biblical version:

Herodias as a medieval goddess of witchcraft, aka Aradia.

Aradia was the primary figure in folklore book called "Gospel of the Witches", which is believed to be a genuine religious text used by a group of pagan witches in Tuscany. Some versions say Aradia was sent to earth to teach oppressed peasants the art of witchcraft to use against the Roman Catholic Church.

Aradia is one of the driving forces behind the "neopaganism" modern day movement. Some Wiccan traditions use the name Aradia as one of the names of the Great Goddess, Moon goddess, or "Queen of the Witches".

According to some teachings, the sexual act becomes not only an expression of the Divine life force, but an act of resistance against all forms of oppression and the primary focus of ritual. This reminds me of kundalini and prana (life force breathing) and the goddess Kaali.

Where is Herodias for you? How witchy are you? How do you connect with your inner goddess? If conjunct natal Mercury, speaking into existence. If this asteroid squares the Nodes, it's possible a person used the craft unethically in a past life and should investigate healing that generational smudge. Break free of generational karma.

Asteroid Dione- Deep Dive

106 Dione: was said to have been the mother of Aphrodite, the Greek goddess of love and beauty. She was an oracle and was worshipped alongside Zeus at the earliest oracle in Greece that was located at Dodona. The priestesses and prophetesses at her shrine in Dodona were called Pleiades or the Doves, which was the sacred bird of her daughter, Aphrodite.

Some call her the goddess of eroticism and fertility. We know she is a great "mother goddess" who can heal immortals with her bare hands. She has strong prophecy and oracle abilities tied to magic, mystery and mysticism.

"Dione wiped away the oozing ichor (divine blood) from Aphrodite's wounded wrist and tried to comfort the sobbing goddess. Dione sought to make Aphrodite realize that even though she was immortal, she was still subject to pain and injury. When Dione spoke to Aphrodite, she revealed priceless information about the vulnerabilities of the Immortals."

~ *Internet Source: mythagora.com*

Keywords: Dione is quick to bring us back to reality, there is no such thing as the easy way out. Fight your battle; heal your wounds and move on. Mystics; healers; spiritual guide; prophetic abilities.

Baby Eve and Asteroid Klonios — Case Study

Baby Eve is the first known human clone, born in 2002, who reportedly, lives in Isreal. She was the product of a company called "Clonaid". Baby Eve's chart is based off the announcement from CNN that she had just been born via cesarean and has a Rodden A rating.

This section will break down a human clone chart with asteroids. For more information about Baby Eve, check the internet to see the many controversial issues her "creation" has captured.

Baby Eve with asteroids:

22199 Klonios: which means to clone or to copy is at 24 Libra. It forms a grand air trine with her 12th house Uranus in Aquarius (secretive, radical science) and Saturn in Gemini (duplication/experimentation). Asteroid Klonios squares natal Mercury in her 11th House, indicating her creation is not in good reception to the masses.

3313 Mendel: father of genetics and labs (scientific laboratories) is-conjunct her natal Sun and Midheaven.

Literal interpretation: genetically created in a lab for scientific advancements.

55555 DNA: in opposition to natal Uranus in Aquarius. Trine to Mendel, the father of genetics. Showing the usage of DNA in a lab environment. It is squaring asteroid Chimera, indicating multiple attempts with techniques.

623 Chimera: at 25 Taurus on fixed star Algol. In mythology, the chimera was a hybrid creature of mixed parts. Sort of like Frankenstein. Or a lab rat. Fixed star Algol is the Medusa star. Medusa is linked to an "altered appearance" out of your control. What many people may not realize is that "chimeric medicine" is what is used to treat cancer and a plethora of other autoimmune diseases. *In medicine, it refers to a person, organ, or tissue that contains cells with different genes than the rest of the person, organ, or tissue. For example, a chimeric antibody is made by joining antibody genes from two different species, such as humans and mice.*

Notice how asteroid Chimera is the apex of a T-square, between her natal Uranus in Aquarius (radical science) and natal DNA? Her natal Moon is trine in with good reception of this energy, indicating success. It is possible that the T-square explains multiple attempts had to be made before one finally was successful. Her Moon says she was the survivor. Eve will be under observation for the rest of her life. Look at her Moon T square to Mendel and Saturn. Older men of science will be her handlers for life.

743 Eugenisis: "good creation" or "good beginnings". The idea of eugenics is based on the principle of being born well with good genes. Selective genetics. The practice aims to improve the genetic quality of the human population.

In Baby Eve's natal chart, asteroid Eugenisis is at 5 Sagittarius, exact conjunct her natal South Node.

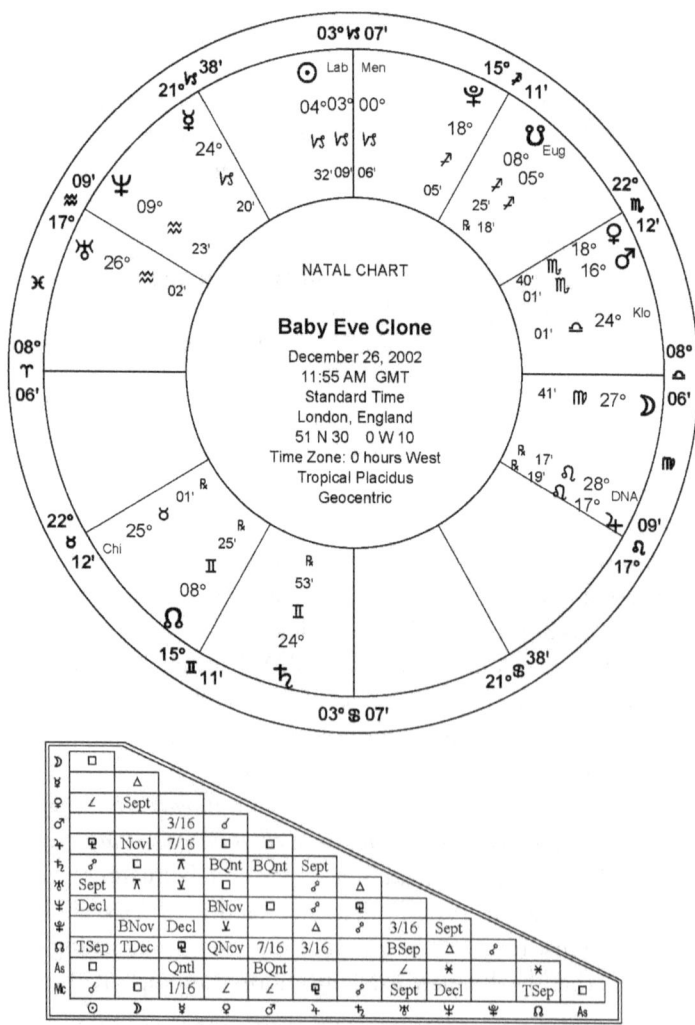

Asteroids in Astrology Simplified 173

Personal	Name	Asteroids
Adam 6461	Bonnie 5947	Clayton 4564
Adams 1996	Bradley 2383	Colby 5569
Adelaide 525	Brady 7691	Cole 5635
Adele 812	Brenda 1609	Coleman 11821
Adriana 820	Brennan 16053	Collins 6471
Aisha 3584	Brett 6179	Connors 13700
Aletheias 259	Brian 2683	Corbin 4008
Alex 3367	Brittany 51599	Cordelia 2758
Alley 14182	Brock 95793	Courtney 30162
Amanda 725	Brody 9974	Crowley 28794
Amber 2933	Brooks 2773	Curtis 3621
Amelia 986	Bryan 2488	
Amy 3375		Dalton 12292
Andersen 2476	Camelia 957	Danae 61
Anna 265	Campbell 2761	Daniel 2589
Annalisa 20014	Candace 4899	Daphne 41
Annette 2839	Carmen 558	Darius 7210
Armando 14572	Carol 2214	Davis 3638
Ashley 6752	Carolina 235	Dawn 1618
Audry 4238	Carolyn 4446	Dawson 1829
Autumn 5461	Carson 6572	Dean 333089
Avery 3580	Cassidy 3382	Deborah 541
	Charlene 5878	Delia 395
Bailey 449922	Charlotte 543	Delores 1988
Baker 2549	Chloe 402	Delphine 3218
Barbara 234	Christa 1015	Demitra 240022
Barry 1703	Christian 192158	Denise 667
Bella 695	Christine 628	Denny 23257
Bertha 154	Christy 129564	Devin 333018
Bianca 218	Clara 642	Diana 78
Blackburn 33550	Claudia 311	Diego 269300

Personal	Name	Asteroids
Dolores 1277	Fabian 25157	Gwyn 358367
Don 4689	Fanny 821	
Donna 3085	Fantasia 1224	Hal 9000
Doris 38	Fay 4820	Halley 2688
Dorothea 339	Felicia 294	Hank 4582
Douglas 2684	Felix 1664	Hanna 1668
Duncan 2753	Francis 2050	Harold 353677
Dweight 92579	Frank 4546	Harriett 1744
	Freda 1093	Harris 2929
Edith 517	Fredrick 41943	Harrison 4149
Edmond 12533	Frieda 722	Harvey 4278
Edwin 1046		Hazel 3846
Eileen 11836	Gabriella 355	Heath 8110
Elaine 1329	Gaby 1665	Heather 3922
Elisa 956	Galle 2097	Heidi 2521
Elizabetha 412	Garcia 4442	Helina 1075
Ella 435	Garrett 28475	Henry 1516
Ellen 2735	Gary 4735	Hilda 153
Elliot 3193	Genevieve 1237	Hillary 3130
Elsa 182	George 3854	Holly 19955
Elvis 17059	Georgia 359	Howard 12561
Emilia 85564	Gerhard 7215	
Emma 283	Gertrud 710	Imelda 34919
Eric 4954	Giada 6877	Irene 14
Erika 636	Giannna 10892	Iris 7
Erin 2167	Gisela 352	Irma 177
Esteban 16641	Gladys 3909	Isabella 210
Esther 622	Gloria 34047	Ivanka 8573
Ethel 2032	Grant 3154	
Eva 164	Grimm 6912	Jackson 2193
Evelyn 503	Guinvere 2483	Jaqueline 1017

Personal	Name	Asteroids
James 2335	Katharina 320	Leona 319
James Bond 9007	Kathleen 3754	Leonard 53435
Jan 389370	Kathryn 2612	Leroy 93102
Jana 8556	Kathy 4711	Lester 14583
Janelle 20673	Kelley 4477	Lewis 4796
Jasmine 28794	Kelly 22312	Leyla 3397
Jason 6063	Kelsey 6260	Libby 5672
Jeanne 1281	Kendra 33898	Lilliana 756
Jenkins 28603	Kendrick 25704	Linda 7169
Jennifer 6249	Kennedy 7166	Lionel 9504
Jenny 607	Kenny 10107	Lisbeth 5320
Jerome 1414	Kent 28346	Lois 2210
Jessie 10464	Kevin 23739	Lola 463
Jo-Ann 2316	Kinsey 31682	Lopez 4657
Joan 2677	Kira 1156	Loretta 1939
Jocelyn 25415	Kirby 51985	Lorraine 1114
Jody 4083	Kitty 9563	Louise 2556
Johanna 127	Kristen 183560	Lottie 3489
Johhny 3252	Kristina 4038	Lucas 9349
Johhny Cash 10505		Lucy 32605
Johnson 5905	Lala 26973	Luisa 599
Jones 3152	Lana 6892	Lydia 110
Jose 1423	Larry 1281	Lynnette 157332
Josephina 303	Laura 467	Lynn 4358
Joyce 5418	Laurel 2865	
Judith 664	Lawrence 4969	MacKenzie 6204
Julia 89	Lee 3155	Madeline 2569
Juliana 816	Lena 789	Mallory 6824
	Leonard 53435	Manuel 12777
Karen 2651	Leonardo 3000	Marc 71445
Kate 2156	Lennon 4147	Marcia 269484

Asteroids in Astrology Simplified

Personal	Name	Asteroids
Marco 55845	Miguel 171396	Nora 783
Marcus 369088	Mika 4557	Noreen 42073
Margo 1175	Mila 3231	Norma 555
Margret 1410	Mildred 878	Norman 16707
Maria 170	Miles 4119	
Marianna 602	Miller 1826	Old Joe 10515
Marilyn 1486	Mimi 1127	Olga 304
Mario 12931	Mira 3633	Oliver 2177
Marion 506	Miriam 102	Olivia 835
Marjorie 4064	Miss Judy 112483	Ophelia 171
Mark Twain 2362	Monica 833	Owen 164792
Marlene 1010	Morgan 3180	
Marshall 32279	Morris 3783	Page 71556
Martha 205	Muriel 2982	Pamela 1243
MartinLuther 7100	Murray 941	Paris 3317
Martina 981	Myra 33799	Patrice 1978
Martinez 2075		Patrcia 436
Marvin 4309	Nancy 2056	Patsy 3310
Mary 2779	Nanette 5852	Patterson 2511
Mathieu 1592	Nanna 1203	Paul 3525
Maury 3780	Naomi 6139	Paula 1314
Mavis 1607	Natalie 448	Payton 85386
Maxine 3977	Natascha 1121	Pearce 3304
McAdams 17408	Nguyen 24052	Pearson 29458
McKenna 42531	Nicky 4755	Penelope 201
Melanie 688	Nicole 1343	Penney 12227
Melissa 114738	Nigel 3795	Perry 5529
Melvin 108096	Nikko 1185	Peter 1716
Michael 1348	Nina 779	Pippa 648
Michela 1045	Nolan 9537	Polina 4780
Michelle 1376	Nonna 4022	Polly 5278

Personal	Name	Asteroids
Poppy 355657	Rosa 223	Shane 1994
Preston 3792	Rosalia 314	Shannon 18838
Pricilla 2137	Rosanna 79240	Sharon 3694
	Rosaparks 384996	Sheldon 201372
Quincy 4372	Rosemary 2057	Shelly 17280
	Roxanne 317	Shelton 5953
Rachele 674	Roy 14533	Shirley 5624
Ralph 5051	Rubin 5726	Sierra 12598
Ramirez 3926	Ruby 2474	Simmons 22294
Randi 3163	Russ 69311	Simone 54983
Rayjay 4668	Russell 1762	Sinatra 7934
Raymond 197189	Rusty 17033	Siri 332
Rebekka 572	Ruth 798	Skip 1884
Regge 3778	Ryan 21936	Smith 3351
Regina 285		Sofia 239672
Reid 3422	Sabina 28887	Sophia 251
Remy 14683	Sabine 665	Spencer 117329
Reseda 1081	Sabrina 2264	Stacey 13389
Rey 13647	Samantha 3147	Stanley 9626
Reyes 14684	Smara 26922	Steven 38540
Reynolds 12776	Samra 12577	Stevin 2831
Richard 3972	Samuel 11622	Steward 15371
Rita 1180	Samuels 38639	Stewart 26712
Roberta 335	Sanchez 14613	Stone 5841
Roberts 3428	Sandra 1760	Sturst 3874
Robertson 360037	Sara 533	Suess 12002
Robyn 5183	Sasha 3680	Sylvia 87
Roderick 16194	Scott 876	Sylvester 13658
Rodriguez 13760	Sean 7051	
Rogers 7894	Seth 86551	Tamara 326
Roman 2516	Shakespeare 2985	Tammy 3403

Personal	Name	Asteroids
Tanner 13668	Wallace 21903	
Tanya 2127	Walsh 7398	
Tara 5863	Walter 8021	
Tatum 3748	Wanda 1057	
Taylor 2603	Warren 5597	
Teresa 11350	Wendy 2993	
Terry 21952	White 10730	
Thalia 23	Wilhelmina 392	
Thomas 2555	William 270373	
Thompson 25166	Williams 1763	
Tina 1222	Wilson 2465	
Toni 924	Wren 3062	
Toya 6990	Wylie 126444	
Tracie 3532		
Tremaine 3806	Young 2165	
Trevino 13716	Yvette 1340	
Tristan 1966		
Trudie 22900	Zachery 104052	
Tucker 10914		
Tyler 113333		
Tyson 13123		
Vernon 6518		
Veronika 612		
Victoria 12		
Viola 1076		
Virginia 50		
Vivian 1623		
Wade 4710		
Wagner 3992		

www.ingramcontent.com/pod-product-compliance
Lightning Source LLC
Chambersburg PA
CBHW060348190426
43201CB00043B/1763